MARK WAUGH ON TOUR
WITH THE AUSTRALIAN CRICKET TEAM
A YEAR TO REMEMBER

MARK WAUGH ON TOUR
WITH THE AUSTRALIAN CRICKET TEAM

A YEAR TO REMEMBER

MARK WAUGH WITH GRANTLEE KEIZA

RANDOM HOUSE
AUSTRALIA

Published by
Random House Australia Pty Ltd
20 Alfred Street, Milsons Point, NSW 2061
http://www.randomhouse.com.au

Sydney New York Toronto
London Auckland Johannesburg
and agencies throughout the world

First published 1997
Copyright © Mark Waugh and Grantlee Keiza

All rights reserved. No part of this publication may be reproduced, stored in a retrieval system, or transmitted in any form or by any means, electronic, mechanical, photocopying, recording or otherwise, without the prior written permission of the Publisher.

National Library of Australia
Cataloguing-in-Publication Data

  Waugh, Mark
  A year to remember: on tour with the Australian cricket team.

  ISBN 0 09 183637.9.

  Waugh, Mark. 2. Cricket – Tournaments – Australia. 3. Cricket players – Australia. I. Keiza, Grantlee. II. Title.

Text Design by Michael Killalea
Picture Section by Associated Press
Typeset by Asset Typesetting Pty Ltd
Printed by Griffin Press, Adelaide

10 9 8 7 6 5 4 3 2 1

Contents

Introduction

1	The Fast Men	1
2	The First Test—The Gabba	9
3	The Second Test—The SCG	19
4	The Third Test—The MCG	27
5	The Fourth Test—Adelaide Oval	33
6	The Fifth Test—The WACA	41
7	Australia v. West Indies	51
8	The Art of Touring	61
9	Enter South Africa	65
10	The First Test—The Wanderers	79
11	The Second Test—St Georges Park	93
12	The Third Test—Centurion Park	105

13	The One-dayers	113
14	Australia v. South Africa	125
15	The Ashes Tour	141
16	The First Test—Edgbaston	157
17	The Second Test—Lords	171
18	The Third Test—Old Trafford	185
19	The Fourth Test—Headingley	197
20	The Fifth Test—Trent Bridge	211
21	The Sixth Test—The Oval	221
22	All Good Things	231
23	Australia v. England	234

Introduction

> 'I love sport. If I was Shane Warne or Dennis Lillee or Mark Waugh it would be a dream.'
>
> MEDIA PROPRIETOR JAMES PACKER

Whether it was taking tea and talking about the punt with Queen Elizabeth II, gang tackling Mal Meninga in a bar at Leeds, being chased by a wild bull elephant in South Africa, listening to my horse race at Harold Park on a mobile phone while sitting in the toilets at Nottingham or taking on Curtly Ambrose in a crucible, it was certainly an exciting year for me and the Australian cricket team.

Since 1989, when a side that the storm-troopers of the British press tagged as the worst to leave Australia whipped the Poms 4–0, we have gradually been rebuilding our place as the best Test cricket side in the world. Under Allan Border and now Mark Taylor, the Australian team has developed into a great side; well-balanced, well-trained, tough, fit, and determined. Australia has now won the Ashes five times in a row 4–0, 3–0, 4–1, 3–1 and 3–2.

In 1997, Tubby Taylor proved himself to be the toughest

cricketer there is. In England, he dug himself out from under the weight of the world and emerged as an Ashes-winning skipper with incredible guts. In the last year, Tubby reached a personal milestone of leading Australia to consecutive victories over both the West Indies and England, and we downed the formidable South Africans in both the Tests and one-dayers.

During the last 12 months, we have travelled to some exotic locations and played cricket that was sometimes outstanding, sometimes ordinary, sometimes successful and sometimes catastrophic. We were beaten by Sri Lanka in the World Cup final, spun out on a trap in New Delhi and wiped out at the Oval chasing a pittance against England.

In between, we clocked up about 80,000 Frequent Flyer miles, produced some phenomenal results and won all three Test series against some damned good sides. We beat the West Indies, South Africa and England in the Test matches and that's not a bad year's work. We spent 312 days out of 365 away from home. Even though the constant travel tends to wear you out, there is nothing like the joy of victory to lift the spirits.

This, then, was a year to remember.

The Fast Men

*'Fast bowlers want to slice a batting side open
and watch it bleed.'*

JOHN SNOW

The noon-day sun in Perth scorched everything beneath it like a blow torch. It was as hot as hell and cricket's fiercest demon was cranking up the thermostat, hurling missiles toward me at close to 100 miles per hour. They said it was 42.7 degrees in Perth on the first day of the final Test against the West Indies. But out in the middle it was closer to 50 as I ducked and dived against Curtly Ambrose.

The heatwave blowing off the desert was so intense that I could feel the soles of my feet burning through my cricket boots. The average spectator sitting beside the fan in front of the TV would have had no idea just how hot and uncomfortable it was, lugging around the protective gear needed to combat the Windies speedsters. The gear weighed a ton, and I have to admit that when I met up with Greg Blewett in the middle of the pitch, we both wondered where our next run was coming from.

The rumour doing the rounds in the days before the Perth Test was that Ambrose, who had struggled with a thigh injury on tour, had already packed his bags and wasn't going to play. Like most rumours though, you could take it with a pinch of salt. It was Ambrose loping in to the crease, all right. And he'd brought his bouncer with him.

The duel between fast bowler and batsman is the cornerstone of Test cricket; the battle that elevates it from a pastime to a test of courage and tenacity. As Harold Larwood used to say: the fast blokes are the ones who put dynamite into the game.

Ambrose was like a bear with a thorn in its paw on that Saturday in Perth, 1 February 1997. The Windies had already lost the Test series to us and, despite a final flourish, had been whipped by Pakistan in the one-day series. They were determined to regain some lost pride.

With Australia at 2–7, my survival was essential. And not just for the sake of preserving my wicket either. I had been hit in the head twice by the West Indian fast bowlers during the series, and I was doing my absolute best to avoid direct hit No. 3. It didn't work. I copped one right in the visor of my helmet.

Ambrose and his skipper Courtney Walsh—two of the very best fast bowlers I've ever faced—were bowling at great speed on a wicket with cracks so wide Tony Greig could lose a whole four-wheel drive down them, let alone his keys. And the huge cracks were widening in the hot, dry conditions.

Australia has never beaten the West Indians in Perth. The combination of a very fast wicket and the growing reputation of the venue as an Aussie graveyard combined to make it very daunting for us. Four years earlier in Perth, Ambrose gave us all a torrid time with a burst of machine-gun deliveries that claimed 7–1. That was an electrifying spell that helped earn him the tag from one cricket writer as being the world's premier ear, nose and throat specialist.

From my experience, Ambrose could also induce heart palpitations. Facing him in Perth was just about the most harrowing time I've had in the game because of the wicket, the heat and the fearsome abilities of cricket's premier big man. Though an era passed when Ambrose and Walsh farewelled Australia after the Perth Test, no-one in the Aussie team shed a tear over their departure. We were all glad we'd never see them again on fast Australian wickets.

At 33, Ambrose may have been in the twilight of his career in Perth, but he remained one of the world's truly great fast bowlers, a rare combination of speed and skill who could make life tough for any batsman on any wicket. On a jack-in-the-box wicket like the WACA Ground, his effectiveness multiplied considerably. As silent as Marcel Marceau, he has a run-up and action as poetic as his full name—Curtly Elconn Lynwall Ambrose. The giant speedster is a fearsome sight as his giraffe legs push him forward, the lantern jaw set grim and the telescopic arms whirring at the point of delivery.

No Test batsman worth his pads, protector, thigh pad, chest protector and helmet will ever admit fear. No way. But when you're playing against Ambrose you definitely feel more edgy at the crease than you would if you were facing a medium-pacer in club cricket. A lot more edgy. It's definitely more a case of being on tenterhooks. I won't say you're frightened of getting hit, but you're reminding yourself constantly that if you're not concentrating totally, the guy can do some pretty serious damage to you.

No-one bowls a better first over in Test cricket than Ambrose, and from the moment he sets off, you know it's going to be a struggle trying to keep your wicket intact. You know that from the first ball he's going to be at you; goading you, challenging you, threatening you. He'll be putting on the pressure and making you sweat and work hard for every run. It's intimidating just to watch him, but when you're facing him every muscle, every emotion, every thought is compressed into a total awareness.

At the crease, he's so tall and imposing that when he bowls it's almost as though he's standing on top of you. The red ball coming out of the dark skin of his hand makes it harder to see, and even though he's getting on for a speedster, he showed in Perth that he can still generate as much pace as he could five or six years ago. His performance was a fitting Aussie finale for the big fella.

You rarely get a bad ball off him to hit for four but when you do … well … you just gulp a little bit, knowing the next six are going to be absolute crackers at your throat, rib cage or toes. Although his last spell in Perth was spoiled to some degree by a spate of no-balls, Ambrose proved that if you start knocking a champion there's always a big chance he'll come right back and knock you right out.

The same goes for Walsh. I found him almost as intimidating in the many contests we've had. As soon as he set a short leg and two blokes out on the hook, you knew he was going to bowl short. He could bowl as quick as Ambrose when he wanted to, but most of the time Curtly was a little faster.

They were both very awkward and Walsh was one of those freakish bowlers whose deliveries seemed to defy the laws of physics and actually gather pace off the wicket. With his long arms, whippy action and great bouncer, Walsh was a tremendous rival. He had the precise control of a surgeon. You rarely got a half-volley off him and almost never a ball wide enough to cut. And like that brand of paint he kept on keeping on. Even with a crook hamstring in Perth, he kept plugging away, over after over. He would plough out a trench with his approach to the crease as he ran in, and in, and in, all day long. He was the sort of workhorse any team from any era would have been proud to call their own.

I've been taking on Courtney Walsh for years. In only my second game in the Caribbean he hit me in the head with one of his fast, lifting deliveries. I went on to make 108, but the Jamaicans enjoyed the blow to my head much more than the century. Jamaica can be a very intimidating place. So can Perth. But the combination of the WACA wicket and the West Indian fast bowlers wasn't our only experience with some ferocious pace last summer.

During the 1996–97 season, Australia also played host to two of the other big guns of the fast-bowling war machine, Pakistan's Wasim Akram and Waqar Younis, here for the Carlton and United one-day series. The performances of these two over the years have put them alongside the greatest fast bowlers in history.

Akram is the left-handed magician, as cunning in his craft of fast bowling as Shane Warne is with his leg spinners. Akram is more of a skidder than Ambrose. He bowls with a flat trajectory but he can still bowl as lethal a bouncer as anyone. I remember him giving it to Tubby Taylor on his first tour of Australia and he gave my brother Stephen a pretty good work-out in Rawalpindi in 1994. He said it was the fastest and most dangerous spell he's ever faced.

Akram is the most gifted of any fast bowler I've faced. He has every trick in the book and a couple that haven't been written down yet. He can do anything with the ball. He can swing it, he can bowl fast, he can bowl bumpers or yorkers. He can go over the wicket or around the wicket. And being a leftie gives him an extra angle to work with, and another degree of difficulty for the batsmen.

Waqar Younis, master of the in-swinging yorker, has been Akram's partner in crime against batsmen for years. He is a pretty unnerving sight, charging into the crease with that big barrel-chested approach and wind-up. He's not as fast as he used to be when he tore into the Aussies as a 19-year-old, but he can still wipe out a side on his day.

For decades, Pakistan were famished in the fast bowling stakes, with a stiff and medium-fast seamer in Sarfraz Nawaz, their most dangerous front man. Now they turn out fast bowlers like the Japanese turn out cars. In Hobart we got to see another of their potential match winners in Mohammad Zahid. Twenty years old and bloody sharp. He's only skinny, but he has a whippy action and genuine pace. He doesn't have the control yet and could go for a lot of runs, if not on song. It's fairly easy to play a one-day game every two weeks. But the rigours of a Test match day in and day out can be a gruelling exam on the mental discipline of a fast bowler. Only time will tell if Zahid has the goods.

In South Africa, later in 1997, Australia would also battle with a couple of genuine speedsters in Allan Donald and Lance Klusener, while Brett Schultz came in to ignite the fireworks for a rare South African celebration at the end of the series. In England we'd renew our acquaintance with perhaps the fastest of them all,

Devon Malcolm, and his two trusty sidekicks, Darren Gough and Andy Caddick.

When it came to pacemen, Australia came to the fore in 1996–97. We uncovered the pony-tailed express, Jason Gillespie, who established himself as the fastest bowler in Australia. And, more importantly, we also saw the continued rise and rise of a big-hearted bushie who made headlines and broke records all year. A deadly accurate fast man who put in some astonishing performances in what became a year to savour.

The First Test—The Gabba

'It's simple. I just tuck him up for a while from round the wicket, then give him the one outside off stump and he can't resist it.'

GLENN MCGRATH ON HOW TO DISMISS BRIAN LARA

Glenn McGrath has travelled a long way since he drove his $8000 Commodore down from the farm at Narromine to Sydney. For 450 kilometres, his mum followed in the family car, towing a caravan behind her that would be Glenn's home for 13 months as he strove to make it as a top-class cricketer. These days, Glenn travels the world as one of cricket's premier fast bowlers. He's given up the van for a flash joint by the beach at Cronulla and he gets around in a Saab convertible.

He was Australia's match winner in the series against the West Indies; the bloke who helped silence the screaming talents of Brian Lara and the man who gave us a warhead to compete with Ambrose and Walsh. He was the man who helped restore some of the bruised pride we had suffered in our winter of discontent leading up to the West Indies' tour down-under in 1996–97.

In the World Cup final in Lahore in March, 1996, Sri Lanka

beat us convincingly after we had fought desperately to make the final. The one-time stragglers of world cricket had emerged with bats blazing, redefining the concept of the limited-overs game. Seven months later, at the Feroz Shah Kotla Stadium in Delhi, they defeated us again in a morale-sapping three and a bit days of humidity and humiliation. I am still at a loss why the Australian Cricket Board sent us over there for one Test. It was a tough ask. In a one-off Test you have one bad day and that's it. You just can't come back.

Greg Baum of the Melbourne *Age* wrote that the ground in Delhi, 'with its weed-strewn terraces and grotesque concrete grandstand, its wreath of smog and its shroud of dust, looked to the Australians a likely place for a calamity'.

So it proved to be. The pitch was as dry and dusty as the grandstand, which is not a slight on those responsible for its preparation, but rather praise. They had created a work of art on which their masterful spinners could wipe the canvas with us. We didn't have Shane Warne to fire back. Peter Willey, the umpire and one-time English spinner, reckoned it was the worst first-day pitch he'd ever seen and took a piece home with him to England to prove it. Eventually, we lost by seven wickets on a pitch that displayed more tricks than an Indian snake-charmer.

Psychologically, we were at a low ebb as we geared up to meet the West Indies in a five Test series at home and joined Pakistan in a three-way Carlton and United one-day series. Defeat in Delhi had left us all feeling crook in the guts and after our 1995 series triumph in the West Indies—the first by a visiting team in 22 years—showed how quickly the game can change.

As you can imagine, we were eager to quickly re-establish a

THE FIRST TEST—THE GABBA

winning platform from the First Test against the Calypso boys in Brisbane. And it wasn't long before big Glenn, the farm boy from Narromine who developed his pace bowling beside his old man's machinery shed, proved himself to be our match winner, eventually being named Man of the Series. He troubled the record-breaking Lara every time he bowled to him. From the First Test in Brisbane, Glenn had the wood on his big-name rival.

In five Tests, Glenn took 26 wickets for the series. In the first six times Lara was dismissed, Glenn picked him up five times. Really, that statistic isn't all that surprising when you consider that Glenn is our best fast bowler and he stuck to a very effective plan of cramping Lara for room and frustrating him at every opportunity. I think once he took Lara's wicket a couple of times it became a mental barrier for Brian that he found very difficult to overcome.

As a paceman, Glenn had improved out of sight in the year leading up to our 1996–97 series against the Windies. I compare him favourably with Curtly Ambrose in terms of style, though he has not yet developed into quite the same category of fast bowler. Against the Windies, he bowled well within his capabilities but when he needed to, he could generate good pace. He has a good bumper and was always at the Windies batsman.

Glenn developed his fast bowling on his father's farm, having to navigate a fence in his run-up and switching from a cricket ball to a tennis ball for safety reasons when night began to fall. Like a lot of teenagers in the country, he found it tough to get work at Narromine. He couldn't land an apprenticeship in carpentry and ended up working as a labourer on a cotton farm and then joined the State Bank in Narromine.

He had trouble getting a bowl for his local Backwater Cricket

Club under-16s side, but when he was 19, Dougie Walters, the great Test batsman and talent scout, spotted him in action and encouraged Glenn to try his luck in Sydney. With an invitation from former Aussie keeper Steve Rixon to play for Sutherland, Glenn headed for Sydney with his mum as support.

He made his home at Ramsgate Beach Caravan Park for 13 months. He was known as 'Millard' for a while, after the brand of van. He's now more often known as 'Pigeon', for his thin build, and 'Norman', as in Norman Bates, the quiet killer from Hitchcock's movie *Psycho*.

Over the years, Glenn has ditched a lot of his country ways and when he steps out these days, he looks very much like the city slicker. But despite the trappings of the big smoke, Pigeon will always be a farm boy at heart. He's always reading those stupid magazines on hunting and shooting and a few years ago in Pakistan when all the players were asked to bring a video for entertainment, he pitched in with *Hunting and Skinning Wild Pigs*—45 minutes of filleting fun that went down like the *Titanic*.

Glenn recently bought a big property out the back of Bourke with the money he is making from Test cricket and you can guarantee that no wild pig in the area will be safe from now on. Given the rush of blood he's been experiencing over the last couple of years, the world's batsmen are all in trouble, too.

The pitch in Brisbane for the first day of the First Test against the West Indies was encouraging for their fast bowlers, operating before a crowd of just on 17,000—the biggest crowd at the Gabba in 20 years. We quickly forgot the nightmare of India because we had new horrors to contend with.

THE FIRST TEST—THE GABBA

Courtney Walsh won the toss and put us in to bat and then the fun and games started against Walsh and Ambrose at top pace on a lively wicket. Matthew Elliott made his debut in this match after scoring 158 in the Australia A game against the Windies in Hobart a week earlier. Matthew Hayden had made 224 in that match but Elliott was probably preferred for the First Test because of the way he had made his runs in that game and the style he had been showing all summer.

Before the match Mark Taylor took Matty aside and told him it was just another Test match and Shane Warne tried to put him at ease by giving up his single room and sharing with the new boy. Shane, Tubby, Geoff Marsh, and our physiotherapist Errol Alcott all took him out for dinner on the night before the Test and told him about their experiences in Test cricket. That seemed to settle Matt's nerves for a while but about 20 minutes before the match started he turned to Warney and said: 'Jeez, I thought I was going really well but now my legs won't stop shaking.' I know the feeling. Although my legs might not shake as much as they did once, sometimes—even with 60 or more Test matches behind me—I'll be walking out to the crease with the jitters, feeling as though my balance just isn't quite right.

In any case, Matt carried his nerves out to the middle and joined some pretty illustrious company including Graham Gooch, Michael Atherton, Victor Trumper and Syd Gregory as players who made nought on debut. He looked unlucky to be given out, though. It was not the ideal start to his Test career, but as he showed over subsequent months, he is a class player. More than one commentator has pointed out the physical and style similarities between him and Bill Lawry and hopefully that inauspicious debut in Brisbane was the start of great things for him. There were just four runs on the board when Matt departed, thanks to the combination of Ambrose, wicket-keeper Courtney Browne, a green track, and a new ball. It would be another 135 runs before the Windies would get another victim.

Little did Mark Taylor know that the 43 he made before his wicket was shattered by Walsh would be his biggest score for seven months. Little did Ricky Ponting know when he was out for 88 that he'd get just one more Test before being dropped. 'Punting' Ponting is a gambling man like me. He's especially into the dogs and he has one called Elected down in Tassie that has won 22 races and is a star performer in Launceston. He took his chances in Brisbane, playing his shots, including a towering six off Kenny Benjamin. He had a bit of luck go his way, too, his first four coming off the edge and surviving a dropped catch on 81, but it wasn't an easy track to bat on.

Benjamin was a surprise packet for the Windies, underrated a little as a fast bowler, but deceptively quick and a good swinger of the ball. In Brisbane, he bounced a ball into me that didn't rise the way I expected it to and it hit the back of my head at the base of the helmet. It meant the ball whacked half of my head as well. It was a pretty nasty knock. Every time I get a headache I'll probably remember the one Kenny Benjamin gave me.

You can end up with a huge headache taking on the fast bowlers and that one was pretty bad. What hurt even more was when I hooked a ball from Walsh into the gloves of Courtney Browne. Browne dropped a few sitters during the Tests but he held onto this one long enough to have me trudging off. When Michael Bevan was out the very next ball we were 5–196 and Walsh looked an even-money bet to repeat the hat-trick he notched at the Gabba in 1988.

But no-one figured on Ian Healy.

Heals went into the match under a little of the pressure that Mark Taylor would face for the next six months. There were plenty of people in the press calling for his head and for the stylish Adam Gilchrist to take the wicket-keeping spot. I suppose Heals felt the pressure after having suffered a hamstring injury in India and with Gilchrist in top form. But really, I don't see why Heals was subjected to so many attacks. While Adam is a tremendous striker of the ball, Heals really has no rival when it comes to wicket-keeping and he came out in Brisbane and showed everyone what he could do with the bat when the team really needed it. He scored a superb, unbeaten 161 that shattered the confidence of the Windies and broke their spirit.

No wonder on Day 2 the Brisbane crowd started singing 'Waltzing Matilda' to cheer Heals. His chanceless innings was the highest score recorded by an Australian wicket-keeper in the 120-year history of Test cricket and the first century at the Gabba by a Queensland-born player. Remarkable, considering the fact that it was made after he came to the crease with Courtney Walsh on a hat-trick and against an attack that also included Ambrose, Bishop, Benjamin and Hooper. That's not bad opposition.

It was an innings of fight rather than finesse. As Peter Roebuck summed it up: 'Healy scores runs at the vital times and is an undiluted team man. He plays like a handy cricketer and has the record of a great one.' Heals answered his detractors as well as any cricketer has in history. Because of his enormous innings—well supported by Stephen's 66—Australia made 479, which the

Windies were always going to struggle to match. The West Indian reliance on speed with a lack of variety really told. It was the fifth time in their last six Tests that they had conceded more than 400 runs.

All 11 Australian fielders came out for the West Indian innings wearing the traditional baggy green cap and we were determined that everyone in the side would have a part in our united effort to dismantle them. It was a show of solidarity against a team with an abundance of flair but little discipline. After I picked up Lara off McGrath, the Windies were 3–77 and it was only through the stroke play of the erratic but often brilliant Carl Hooper and the tenacity of Shivnarine Chanderpaul that they ended up making 277, more than 200 runs behind.

Hooper's a very gifted player, but his Test record should be much better than it is. He often batted brilliantly in the one-day internationals on the 1996–97 tour and scored a sometimes elegant century at the Gabba. However, in 18 previous Tests against us he had never scored more than 64 and was averaging just 21 runs an innings. He's a player who often gets out in funny ways, though I'm sure he doesn't get the joke.

In Brisbane, Hooper was looking pretty menacing as he neared his century until Tubby decided to blow his confidence all the way down Vulture Street. Stephen, while not being the greatest bowler in the world, seems to have a thing over Hooper. Again I think it's largely a mental thing. Stephen had picked him up five times and probably that played a bit on Hooper's mind. Big Carl's confidence ebbed away as soon as Stephen, with a glint in his eye, took the ball.

Hooper lashed at everything in the 90s and on 99 charged down

THE FIRST TEST—THE GABBA

the wicket in a desperate run to reach his century. Glenn McGrath knocked over the stumps with a throw as straight as a rifle barrel. It took eight replays before third umpire Peter Parker gave Carl the green light. But the damage to the big Guyanan was done. Two overs and two runs later, Ponting scooped up a great catch down the leg side to send Hooper and the West Indian hopes of a revival on their way. At that stage they were 4–249 but, as happened so often during their series, their tail didn't so much wag as drop off. They lost seven wickets for 28 runs in just 12 overs.

Chanderpaul was dropped on 81, but I caught him off Paul Reiffel's bowling on 82. In an innings that became typical of his series he batted solidly without going that one step further to a really big score. I thought Chanderpaul was the best of the West Indian batsman on this tour—certainly the most difficult to get out. He is a slim little bloke who had problems with cramping because of his slight frame, problems with infected wisdom teeth and problems cracking three figures. We played on that mental barrier as much as we could, pressuring him into mistakes, and it would be a few months after he left Australia when he finally made a century.

The Windies' first innings was also notable for the groin strain Stephen suffered while bowling. The injury kept him out of the next Test and gave Greg Blewett a welcome recall to the team. The injury also allowed Ponting to bowl out the rest of Stephen's over. He picked up the prized scalp of Jimmy Adams l.b.w. and would have figures of 1–0 for the series, bringing his Test bowling tally to two wickets at an average of four. Phenomenal if he can maintain it! Tubby decided not to enforce the follow-on but rather bat again to let Shane Warne have last use of the Gabba wicket.

In our second innings I got a half century and Heals hit 45 not out as we set the Windies 420 to win. It was too much for them. Sherwin Campbell batted steadily for his second Test century, keeping his head while everyone else around him was losing theirs, slashing when they should have been solidifying. It took Campbell nearly seven hours to make his 113 before becoming Australia's ninth victim of the innings. His composed effort also saw him pass 1000 runs in Test cricket.

I caught Lara in the slips. He let fly at a ball that McGrath angled across him. McGrath grabbed four wickets and Michael Bevan gave an indication of the dynamic bowling performances he would display in this series by snaring the wickets of Hooper, Bishop and Campbell for 46 runs. Pretty amazing, considering he bowled 86 overs for Yorkshire a few months before to take four wickets for the entire season. Before the season was over, Michael had emerged as one of our most dangerous bowlers.

In the end, we won the First Test by 123 runs with 53 minutes of play to spare. The Windies looked miserable, and their expressions would grow even sadder over the next few weeks as we twisted the knife a little harder.

And Glenn McGrath had tasted blood.

The Second Test—The SCG

'You tell that Healy he is not welcome in our dressing-room again.'

BRIAN LARA TO AUSTRALIAN TEAM MANAGER GEOFF MARSH AFTER BEING DISMISSED, CAUGHT BEHIND

I've been a mad keen punter ever since I can remember. When I was a kid, Dad took us to the Bankstown Trots and I must have backed a winner because I've been going back ever since. My success rate hasn't always been as good as that very first time, but when the horses are in your blood they're harder to dismiss than my brother Stephen once he's settled in at the crease. Racing is a great escape from cricket and I'm in my own little world at the track. Whenever I can, I get to the Canterbury races or the trots at Bankstown and Harold Park. Along with golf, the horses are my favourite pastime; the form guide my favourite reading.

Cricket and racing have always gone hand in hand. Keith Miller loved Randwick and Ascot as much as he did the SCG and Lord's. I remember playing exhibition matches in the country with Dougie Walters and he'd come back with tickets for a million small bets in his wallet. The biggest punt I've had was when a grey called Manribo won in Melbourne at long odds. I had $300 on him and had tipped him to everyone at the Revesby TAB.

Racing has only got in the way of my cricket once. I backed Super Impose when it won the Cox Plate at 25–1 over the favourite Naturalism in 1992. I was playing for Bankstown against Sydney Uni and we needed 30 runs to win and they were about to jump at Moonee Valley. I had to go and watch that race. Stephen and I were batting and our side were home and hosed. I had $200 on Super Impose and I just couldn't miss it. I went for a big hit and top edged the ball straight up in the air and I got to see my long shot bring home the cash.

You beauty, boy.

It's the only time I ever did it. But it wasn't the only time Super Impose finished in front.

I owned a galloper with Gai Waterhouse called Drive Time for a year, and I bought shares in a pacer called Clever Kiwi, and I also own Moon Boy and Olblico. Glen Frost is the trainer-driver. At one stage, five of us trotting fans whacked in $10,000 each to buy two horses. We were going to buy another one called Low Zingara but were told his legs weren't great. The next week he won a $10,000 race at Moonee Valley. Sometimes you can't pick 'em.

If Matty Elliott was a trotter, you'd make the bloke wear blinkers every time he had a run. At the SCG he ran into me with the force of Dean Pay making a tackle for the Canterbury Bulldogs. And earlier in the season he'd barged straight into his Victorian teammate Warren Ayres. Matt has every shot in the copybook but running between wickets is not his long suit. Our mid-wicket collision at the SCG during the Second Test against the Windies would have been laughable if it hadn't resulted in Matt missing out on his first Test century and having to undergo surgery.

Here's what happened.

It was 15 minutes before lunch in our second innings and Matt was looking pretty good in the mid-70s. He hit a ball from Carl Hooper behind square leg and we took off for a single. We brushed each other going for the first run and as we turned for the second, Courtney Walsh threw the ball to Hooper at the bowler's end. We stepped the wrong way trying to avoid each other and ended up colliding head-on. Bang!

Hooper somehow muffed what was a pretty simple run-out. He let me off the hook and threw to the far end hoping to catch Matt short. But Courtney Brown was too slow getting the bails off. Matt did a Greg Louganis and made a gold-medal winning dive. Maybe Hooper thought I was playing poorly and went easy on me. In any case, it took Matt weeks before he could park himself and his bung knee in front of the television and wince through the replays of us both hitting the deck. Matt ended up needing knee surgery and missed the rest of the series.

It was just one of those freak accidents. For some reason we both changed sides of the wicket at the same time. Matt explained the mishap by saying that he had developed a habit of always turning to the same side and pushing off his right leg, which is his stronger of the two. He said that he remembered spinning in the air, landing on his backside and making a desperate lunge for the crease. At the same time, he realised he'd done some major damage to himself.

He told journalist Linda Pierce, 'I thought [my knee] might have just been locked or something because I tried to move it and just couldn't move it at all. I thought then "nuh, something's wrong here" and that's when the embarrassment took over. I was taken off on this golf trolley by Merv, the room attendant—that was more embarrassing than anything—and as we were going off I had my leg hanging out of the trolley because I couldn't put it on and Merv just missed the gate. I could have actually had my leg taken clean off.'

I've heard about ending up legless after a victory, but that's ridiculous!

The SCG wicket for that Second Test was low and slow and fairly dead. But the game was lively and my mid-wicket crash with Matt was just one of the many incidents that made headlines. The match was characterised by poor fielding from the Windies and the petulance of Brian Lara. In our second innings, when the Windies could have hit us with a double whammy by running me out and having Matt retire hurt, they blew a golden opportunity.

The Windies dropped their heads quite a bit throughout the series when things didn't go their way. Once again they relied on their natural brilliance rather than application and discipline and they paid for it. Ambrose was probably the worst offender, although he still bowled tidily. He can be very lazy in the field and at times looks disinterested, which is strange considering he is such a big-hearted bowler with more than 300 Test scalps to his credit.

The match had started with some good fast bowling from Bishop and Walsh and they had us at 4–94 with me out and before long we were five down. Greg Blewett came into the side to replace Stephen—who'd suffered a groin strain—and he quickly made it obvious that he wanted his recall to be permanent. Greg was dropped twice before he made 69, showing the kind of stroke play

THE SECOND TEST—THE SCG

that helped him become another Aussie record-breaker as the year unfolded. At the other end, Ian Healy was continuing the batting form that had him averaging around 250 and making us all look pretty ordinary. Everyone, that is, except our new batting discovery, Glenn McGrath.

Glenn had the princely average of three as he went out to face the music with Australia at 9–288. Ian Healy whacked on the wicket-keeping pads and we all got ready to take to the field. All out for 290 seemed a fair start, but Big Glenn had other ideas. Pigeon gets stirred a lot over his batting—if batting is what you call it—and he hates the teasing. Believe me, the icy stare that Mike Atherton, Hansie Cronje and Brian Lara have copped over the years has also been wielded on team-mates who make fun of his technique at the crease. Glenn takes his batting very seriously even if no-one else does, maybe even more seriously than he takes his bowling. In any case a few of his dressing-room critics had to eat their words when he finished his innings unbeaten on 24 having put on 43 runs with new boy Jason Gillespie.

Jason came into the side because Paul Reiffel was injured and quickly showed himself to be a speedster of immense hostility and potential. He's a former pizza delivery boy, who hails from my neck of the woods at Bangor, a suburb in the south-west of Sydney, only a lusty six or so from where I grew up at Panania. Dizzy Gillespie had to wait until the West Indies were nearly 300 runs in their first innings before he claimed his first Test scalp in Curtly Ambrose. Despite that, he shows great promise and no doubt there will be many more Test victims ahead.

We had a lead of 27 going into our second innings and set about extending it, with considerable help from sloppy West Indian fielding. Throughout the series the Windies had a lot of problems with their keepers, Browne and Junior Murray. They suffered with dropped catches and this, to some degree, contributed to their decline in morale. Murray slashed his way to some big scores in the Tests and one-dayers by taking his chances with the bat but he was no Ian Healy behind the stumps. And Browne was a funny sort of wicket-keeper in that he'd take some pearlers behind the stumps, spectacular freak catches, and then he'd drop the sitters.

Christopher Martin-Jenkins wrote that Browne 'has a good pair of hands but a man born to keep wicket he clearly is not. His ragged work compounded the felonies being committed all round and inevitably catches were missed—not to mention the simplest of run-out opportunities.'

In my second innings of 67, Browne dropped me before holding one off Ambrose. When he snapped up Michael Bevan off Benjamin for 52, Michael kept looking around to see what happened. Browne had dived full-length to grab a leg glance in one glove, which was pretty amazing from a bloke who at other times seemed to have trouble catching throws from the outfield.

Tubby Taylor declared our innings at 4–312, knowing that the Windies, in their frame of mind, had little chance of getting close. They really looked ordinary in the field at times. A year earlier in Bridgetown, after we'd whipped them inside three days, their then coach Andy Roberts lamented the attitude of some of his players. That slack attitude had followed them to Australia.

Ever the innovator, Tubby tossed me the ball and invited me to open with off-spinners. That's the thing I like about the way Mark plays his cricket. He's willing to take a chance for victory. While he might seem a conservative type of bloke to the public, he's an adventurous captain, much more so than his predecessor Allan Border. I've played for Australia under both and Tubby is a much more personable leader than AB. He'll have a chat to you about your game whereas AB had the attitude that if you were good enough to play for Australia you didn't need much advice. AB would never give his opponents a chance. He would rather go for the draw than take a chance, but Tubby has always been willing to have a go. I guess part of that reason is that AB became captain during a fairly low period in Australian cricket while Tubby inherited a strong team which was more confident of playing aggressively.

The experiment to let me open the bowling was a bold one and it nearly paid off. The ball was turning a bit when I came on and I was disappointed not to have Sherwin Campbell given out. As it was, Warney was getting them to turn a lot more and when he made one spin a good two feet to knock back Chanderpaul's middle stump, the West Indies were done for. Chanderpaul once again was out between 50 and 100, and within two and a half hours Australia won the match by 124 runs to take a 2–0 lead in the series.

In partnership with Carl Hooper, Chanderpaul had given the Windies a sniff of victory, but Warney, McGrath and Bevan squashed their ambition. Lara made just one before he was caught by Heals trying to pull McGrath again and the Windies slumped to 3–33. Lara carried on about the catch. But the umpires had no problem with it. English umpire David Shepherd checked with Darrell Hair at square leg who gave him the nod and sent Lara on his way. 'I saw it straight into Heals' gloves,' Tubby told the press. 'Everyone on the ground thought it was out.'

Heals was unfairly involved in a controversial stumping of Lara four years earlier and the bitterness obviously was still there for Lara. After the dismissal, Lara had the gall to go to the Australian dressing-room while we were all out on the field and tell our coach Geoff Marsh that Heals was no longer welcome in their dressing-room. Heals was disappointed with Lara's reaction, but not surprised. He went to their rooms briefly after the day's play and there was no drama. Lara would have done better to have followed the example of Chanderpaul and concentrate on his batting rather than histrionics.

'Chanderpaul was playing on a rough pitch and he made it look as though it was a road,' Tubby said. Eventually Chanderpaul was run over and we made short work of the last six wickets in the afternoon, taking three of them while the score remained on 176. It was the first time in 21 years that the Windies had lost back-to-back Test matches.

'We dropped too many catches and had too many missed chances,' said Courtney Walsh. 'We thought we had a chance when Chanderpaul and Hooper were batting, but the ball that did Chanderpaul was a gem from Warne, and balls like that will always turn the course of any game.'

Warney passed Clarrie Grimmett's 216 wickets to become Australia's sixth most successful bowler during the course of the match. Michael Kasprowicz had bowled well in his first two Test matches but was yet to celebrate a Test wicket. Glenn McGrath had been voted Man of the Match with seven wickets and quite a few runs. Curtly Ambrose had his feelings hurt. And there's nothing worse than an angry fast bowler with a point to prove.

The Third Test—The MCG

'People figured I'm all washed up. I know I'm not.'

CURTLY AMBROSE

Behold. The giant speaks.

To say the media covering the Third Test were astonished when Curtly Ambrose opened his mouth, is like saying we were a little surprised by Glenn McGrath's batting in Sydney. Curtly has been as difficult to interview over the years as Greta Garbo or Harpo Marx. Most of the West Indian players are difficult to get to know and I don't think even his own team-mates really know what big Curtly is like.

Contrary to their reputation as the party kings of cricket, the West Indians, from my experience, are a fairly aloof bunch. They are from a different culture and while, in the main, they are friendly enough, they tend to mix in their own circles. You don't see them out at night and they pretty much leave straight after the game. At the end of the day's play in the first three Tests we'd have a drink or two with them. They're nice enough guys, but they would do their own thing and not socialise that much with us.

Ambrose, more than any of them, is hard to get to know. He'd often walk past in the nets and not even acknowledge you, not even a nod of hello. I don't know whether it was shyness or what, but he'd keep his head down and walk right by. On this tour he was a little friendlier than usual. Maybe because it was his last tour, he opened up a little more; he acted more human. His interview at the Melbourne Test when he was named Man of the Match was proof of this and he even had a cheesy grin plastered on his head for the Weet-Bix ads. I guess because it was his last tour to Australia he didn't want to leave a bad impression behind him. Or maybe deep down he's just a big softie. Whatever—fast bowlers are a strange breed.

Before the Test match, Curtly had promised his team-mates that he'd get 10 wickets. Less than six hours later, firing them down in front of the biggest Test match crowd in Australia for 25 years, he was halfway there, having taken 5–55. And then, in the words of Melbourne journalist Ron Reed, he 'presented himself for questioning and bared his soul in what might be the most expansive interview he has ever given, certainly in this country'.

It was obvious that Curtly had been stung into action by the criticism heaped on him after the first two Tests. He hadn't bowled too badly, but he had come up short in the wickets department. Just about all the critics were writing him off. Our boys weren't though.

He was, after all, 33 years old, ancient by the rigorous standards of fast bowling, especially given his endless cricketing commitments to the West Indies and Northamptonshire. But in the lead-up to Melbourne, Curtly had shown that the slice of luck he

THE THIRD TEST—THE MCG

needed was starting to go his way. He had worked on a new angle of attack around the wicket and bowled with real fire in a one-dayer against Pakistan at Adelaide.

It might have been Christmas, but there was no cheer from Curtly going into battle at the MCG. 'He is so angry he won't even talk to himself in the shower,' said Colin Croft, one of Curtly's predecessors in the realm of ferocious fast men from the Caribbean. Within the first hour of play, Curtly had dismissed Matt Hayden, Tubby and me. At one stage he had the figures of three wickets for five runs off eight overs. He revealed his motivation later. 'From the time I made my debut for the West Indies,' he said, 'people have been saying things about me. That I'm a has-been, that I'm washed up. It doesn't really bother me. As a matter of fact I thrive on things like that.' Thrive he did.

Curtly was discovered bowling a tennis ball on the beaches of Antigua and has ridden waves of success ever since. But rarely has he ever put on such a command performance as he did before the 72,821 fans at the MCG for the start of the Test match on Boxing Day. They were treated to some glorious cricket from the Windies, the kind of performance that once had them as the unchallenged world champions of the game.

The MCG is one of the great sporting stadiums in the world and to play there before a big crowd is a thrill for any cricketer. To lose there really hurts. The wicket was grassy and played well for the first two days, but was very unpredictable after that.

Matthew Hayden, who has massacred bowlers at first-class level for years, was recalled into the Test team to partner Tubby at the top of the order. Matt had a brief tenure as an Australian opener, scored a Test century in the next match, but was soon relegated back to the confines of first-class cricket, scoring century after century and rueing his lost opportunities at the top level.

Ambrose had the look of Wile E. Coyote about him in Melbourne, drooling at the prospect of getting stuck into the side's newcomers, Hayden and Justin Langer. 'Usually when I see a couple of young faces come into Test cricket I want to make sure I stamp my authority early,' he told reporters later, 'let them know this is the big time. That's one thing that really motivates me.'

Carl Hooper caught Matt in the slips off Ambrose for five, Tubby was bowled and I was l.b.w. Justin, who came in at first wicket down in place of Ricky Ponting, was run out for 12, not long after hooking Kenny Benjamin for six. But Stephen, Greg Blewett and Heals—the leading run-scorer in the series—saved the day, lifting us from 4–27 to all-out 219. Pigeon could not repeat his batting feat from Sydney and was caught by Hooper off Ambrose from a ball that came off his helmet grille. Someone must have teased him about it because Sherwin Campbell copped a fearful bouncer, as fast as Pigeon's ever bowled, and was then l.b.w. two balls later. After two Test defeats, the West Indies finally had a day in which they could stand tall.

Brian Lara vowed to hit a century to complement Ambrose's five wickets. He took 20 minutes to get off the mark, played nervously at three balls from Pigeon and then steered a fourth straight to Warney, waiting with a smile on his face in the gap between second slip and gully. Pigeon had now picked up Lara in four out of five innings.

If McGrath was hostile, then Jason Gillespie was downright homicidal. He only bowled three overs before a side strain crippled him and ended his series. But they were three doses of lightning.

THE THIRD TEST—THE MCG

He bowled one ball which flew over Heals' head and bounced once before it reached the fence. That's fast.

None of the Aussie team were keen to face him in the nets and I know how quick he is. He hit me in the glove once and almost broke a finger. Losing him for the rest of the Test was an even more severe blow, even though Pigeon and Warney managed to contain the Windies to 255.

McGrath described the MCG as having the most fast bowler-friendly wicket in the country and Malcolm Conn wrote in the *Australian* that Lara 'had become so tortured by McGrath on this tour, he will wake up screaming in the middle of the night as dark images of a tall, thin fast bowler bear down on him'.

Pigeon took his best figures for the series of 5–50. He also ran out Carl Hooper and his one-handed caught-and-bowled to get rid of the always-dangerous Chanderpaul was an acrobatic feat that belied his 195-centimetre frame. It was Chanderpaul's first false stroke in three and a half hours at the crease and the man who always seemed to be the hardest West Indian to dismiss was putting one little leg after the other on his way to the dressing-room.

Junior Murray pretended it was a one-day game and hoicked everything while Jimmy Adams held up the other end, never really looking like a bloke once rated the best batsman in the world, but still keeping the bowlers frustrated and the scoreboard attendants in a job. Murray's first two scoring shots were miscued hooks that flew halfway to fine leg. He was eventually out for 53 when he finally hit one in the middle and was caught in the deep.

Adams was not out on 74 at the end of their innings and their slim lead was enough to spark the speedsters into overdrive.

Within three overs, Australia had lost two wickets for three runs with Matt and Justin both getting ducks. With Ambrose taking 4–17 and his 100th Australian wicket in the process, the Windies bowled with a ferocity that had been missing in the two previous games. We were blown away for 122 and they needed less than two hours to score a victory by six wickets

Tubby made 10 in the second innings after having compiled seven in the first. The heat on him started to intensify and he found himself defending his position at the top of the side more and more. 'I'm still thinking positively even though I haven't made a lot of runs,' he said. 'There's been a few things said by former captains which have disappointed me a bit. Everyone has lean trots. I'm not overly worried.'

As the months went by and the runs didn't, Tubby found himself on the back foot more and more. He always handled the situation with composure and dignity, but it was a long and painful grilling.

As the West Indies went out to bat in the second innings at Melbourne, we were all reminded that four years earlier in the corresponding match at the MCG, Warney had taken 7–52 on the last day to give Australia a 139-run victory. Unfortunately for us this time there would be no such heroics. Only Curtly Ambrose, with a grin as wide as Bay 13. Having plenty to say.

The Fourth Test—Adelaide Oval

'We've shown this summer that we just didn't get lucky, that we're a good cricket team.'

MARK TAYLOR AFTER AUSTRALIA WRAPPED UP THE 1996–97 SERIES AGAINST THE WEST INDIES AND PROVED VICTORY IN THE CARIBBEAN TWO YEARS EARLIER WAS NO FLUKE

Sir Donald Bradman once gave me a piece of invaluable advice on batting. 'Don't hit the ball in the air,' he said. 'Hit it on the ground.' As simple as that.

It was the style Sir Donald employed throughout his 20-year Test career with more success than any player before or since. During his career, I think he only hit about three or four sixes the whole time and when you look at his monumental achievements his advice is very sound. It's hard to get out caught when the ball is racing across the outfield.

My meeting with Sir Donald in Adelaide a few years ago was organised by Slazenger, one of my sponsors. The two of us hit it off pretty well and spent about half an hour together chatting about cricket then and now. Sir Donald generally comes to every Test match in Adelaide and occasionally a few of the players get together with him for a few minutes to say hello. Apart from that he pretty much keeps to himself. But his words stay with you for a long time afterward.

No doubt the West Indian batsmen, in total disarray in Adelaide and batting like they were late for an appointment somewhere else, could have done with some similar advice. Some of the shots they played, in one of the most undisciplined displays I've ever seen from a Test team, were straight out of Z-grade cricket.

The Fourth Test in Adelaide was the Test match upon which the whole series hung and it was a massive letdown to both the players and the fans that the Windies turned up apparently with no game plan at all. We led the series 2–1 and they all knew that if they could square the series in the City of Churches we'd have the Devil's own job of staying with them on the speedway wicket at the WACA Ground.

It was such a big game for them and we thought they would be well prepared and really ready to have a go. But our hopes for a good, tough challenge went the same way as the Windies' chances of victory when Curtly Ambrose was ruled out after straining his groin trying to lead their quest for the one-day title. Without Curtly as their torch-bearer, the Windies quickly lost their way. He has been a match winner and bully boy for them on so many occasions and I guess his loss to the team for that match was such a severe psychological blow they couldn't muster the strength to dig in and fight their way out.

Tubby had called our loss in Melbourne 'a minor hiccup' and said he felt it was always going to be a bit of a worry on the MCG because 'of the nature of the pitch'. 'It was always going to suit the West Indies because they play their best cricket on uneven type

THE FOURTH TEST—ADELAIDE OVAL

wickets,' he said. If that was the case it seemed they saved their worst cricket for a very good batting strip in Adelaide. As Australia celebrated its national day, we celebrated one of the easiest days in the field the Windies have ever given us. They were all out for 130 in a bit over three hours and by stumps we were nine runs in front with eight wickets still in hand.

The day started disastrously for the Windies when Sherwin Campbell edged an outswinger from Glenn McGrath without scoring. Adrian Griffith gave Andy Bichel his first Test wicket, when the score dived to 2–22. Andy is a tough customer and a good honest trier who swung the ball and bowled really well for his one wicket in the match. Actually, he could have had Griffith out a few times—including a missed slips chance to Mark Taylor on his fourth ball—before he finally got Griffith with one of his late in-swingers.

Brian Lara was again the chief offender for the Windies, and Robert Craddock reported that his dismissal hit them like a hammer in the head. 'Just when the day was calling for Lara to show some scrap and leadership, his bat resembled a one-wood. He swiped at the first ball from Warne as if he was trying to win a longest drive contest.'

Greg Blewett took the catch at mid-on and Warney gave Lara a round of applause. Two weeks earlier Lara had given Warney a touch-up with some big hitting in the one-dayer at Perth and this was Warney's revenge. Maybe Lara was just in a hurry to get away from Glenn McGrath. Or maybe he was simply having another tantrum since only a week earlier the Windies' team management had refused him a day's leave to have a hit of golf with Nick Faldo in Queensland. 'Lara brought his body to the wicket,' wrote

Simon Hughes, 'but left his brain on the tee.' With Lara out of the way the Windies were 3–45 and soon disintegrated along with their hopes for the series.

While Warney had picked up the prized scalp, Adelaide Oval was the scene for Michael Bevan's arrival as a big-time Test match bowler. He was introduced into the attack in the 14th over as first change ahead of Warney. He bowled four overs before lunch and struggled a bit, conceding 19 runs, but after he got some tucker into him, he turned into a champion. Eventually, he had 4–31 including a spell of 4–1 off 28 balls. His pacey chinamen deliveries ripped apart the tail and killed off any resistance, especially from Junior Murray who threw the bat at everything in the hope of repeating his Melbourne half-century. In the end the Windies were bundled out without having faced 50 overs on a wicket that was brimming with runs. We scored 517 in reply.

And loved every minute of it.

While we had gone into the match with only Pigeon and Andy Bichel as our fast men, the West Indies still backed themselves with a four-man speed attack just as they had done for the previous 20 years. Even with Ambrose and Benjamin injured Ian Bishop bowled well to remove Tubby. Walsh bent his back for the next couple of days, but the Windies just didn't have the personnel to do much damage on that wicket. 'After their embarrassing batting collapse,' Simon Hughes wrote, 'the only way back into the match was to field and bowl with tigerish intensity, but instead the West Indies stumbled about like dozy rhinos.'

Patterson Thompson came into this Test with some big wraps on his pace, but he'd be flat out playing first-grade in Australia. Another new arrival, Cameron Cuffy, bowled steadily at a good

THE FOURTH TEST—ADELAIDE OVAL

clip and dismissed Justin Langer for 19, but he was a long way short of Ambrose and Walsh in both speed and ability. Thompson really looked like an average club cricketer. He showed no discipline whatsoever and displayed very little cricket sense in the field or with the bat.

Having said that, at times he could actually be quite dangerous with the ball. I felt that he could have been given more overs than he was because he could be quite fast and also unpredictable. Like a lot of tearaways, his bowling was all over the shop and hard to pick up. But we did our best to put him away, hitting 80 runs off his 16 overs. That was half the overs that Walsh, Bishop, Cuffy and Carl Hooper were asked to bowl. The Windies' horror match was compounded by three crucial wickets off no-balls and Junior Murray also muffed a catch and a difficult stumping.

Matt Hayden finally got the Test century his enormous potential had been promising for years, snaring 125. Although his ton took Matt the best part of six hours, I don't think he worried too much about the amount of time, only the three figures the scoreboard attendant needed next to his name. Matt had his share of good fortune. He was dropped three times and caught from a no-ball among eight botched chances from the Windies that Greg Baum called 'a slapstick show of lamentable misfielding that harked back to the first two Tests of the series'. But he brought the ton up in style with four boundaries in five balls from Cuffy.

I was out for 82, edging a cut off Hooper onto Murray's thigh, where the keeper managed to snatch the rebound from the flap of his pads. I was filthy getting out that close to a century because there were plenty of runs for the taking and it was not the sort of bowling that should have claimed me for 80-odd. But the bloke I really felt sorry for was Greg Blewett, bowled by Cuffy for 99, in front of his home town fans. Is there any worse feeling in cricket? Getting out for 99 in a Test is like falling off the horse as you lead them home to the finish line in the Melbourne Cup. Like dropping the ball over the line when you're about to score the grand-final winning try.

Blewey got to 50 by top-edging a pull off Cameron Cuffy that Walsh seemed certain to take at mid-on. The skipper dropped it. Tony Cozier said it was 'a moment which, more than all the others, captured the misery of the day'. Blewey was 91 not out overnight, but the next morning some tight bowling kept him on 99 for the first five balls of a Cuffy over. He tried to hit a single off the last, but pushed it back onto off stump and walked off as though there was a hangman waiting for him back in the dressing-room. We finished our innings with Bevvo 85 not out and a lead of 387.

The Windies had already kissed the Frank Worrell trophy goodbye long before they slumped to 2–22 in their second innings thanks to the departure of Griffith and Chanderpaul. Brian Lara didn't exactly fill them with confidence when he made his way to the crease, given the fact that in seven previous Test innings he had scored just 86 runs. But Lara finally came good, hitting Warney and Bevvo for sixes and finishing the day at 65 not out. By that stage the Windies were 6–154.

The next morning, Ian Healy clung on for dear life to Lara's bottom edge off Warney and the Prince was gone for 78. Bevvo quickly mopped up the tail and, with 85 not out and match figures of 10–113, he was also Man of the Match.

Tubby had become the first Australian captain to win two series against the West Indies. 'We've got a strong, talented side and we've played some excellent cricket,' he said. 'The West Indies have based their game plan on four fast bowlers for the last 20 years. We overcame that in 1995 and we've done it again here. I suppose their formula is a bit outdated.'

The Fifth Test—The WACA

'We did not show enough hunger and we didn't show we wanted it as much as the Australian team.'

COURTNEY WALSH, REFLECTING ON A SERIES GONE WRONG

There's only one thing more daunting than facing Curtly Ambrose on a fast track with cracks all through it. It's appearing on 'This Is Your Life'. Only a week before Stephen and I were 'hijacked' by Mike Munro I'd been sitting at home watching the show and telling my fiancee Sue Porter, 'Geez, I'd hate to go on that. The only thing worse would be to get pushed into something on 'Who Dares Wins'.'

The next week, on national television, our lives were flashed before us on the big screen. It was great to be honoured by the program and to catch up with lots of top people we've met over the years, even if it was all a bit of a shock. I'll never forget appearing on the show. But that's it for surprises, thanks very much. If Mike Whitney thinks I'm going to eat worms or go bungee-jumping on his program, he can forget it. I did enough jumping on the WACA ground wicket in Perth against Mr Ambrose and friends when

Stephen and I matched the world record for brothers playing in the same Tests. It was our 43rd Test together, equalling the mark set by Ian and Greg Chappell. Hopefully, we'll push the record much higher over the next few years, but I'm not relishing facing the West Indies in Perth in the year 2001.

When we played the West Indies in 1993, the wicket at the WACA had been very grassy. This time the groundsmen tried to make it with a little less grass and the result was that it was just too dry. The day before the match the pitch already had cracks on it and we knew it would break up, plus extreme temperatures were forecast. Once you have a pitch like that, and you're facing bowlers like the West Indians, the strip becomes virtually unplayable. The ball hits a crack and it can go anywhere; at your toes, at your throat or your rib-cage.

The critics had written Ambrose off, so he came back and made us pay. Ambrose bowled without luck in the first two Tests of the tour and a lot of people were saying he was finished. But in the Melbourne Test, on a pitch which suited him because it was up and down, he bowled with savage pace. In Perth it was much the same, with the wicket becoming a dangerous accomplice: unpredictable and menacing. As soon as Ambrose sniffs a weakness in anyone or thinks the pitch will suit him, he really changes gear and brings a whole new dimension of survival to the game. The Perth wicket suited him.

Before the match Courtney Walsh had lamented the crook state of West Indian batting. 'I don't think we've batted over a day in any of the Test matches,' he said, sadly. 'The batsmen haven't produced consistently at all. Even the Test we won we didn't dominate with the bat. We just didn't get enough runs on the

THE FIFTH TEST—THE WACA

board throughout the series to constantly put Australia under any pressure.' Walsh added that he was very disappointed because the team had played very poorly. 'This is the first series I've played in that we've been so consistently poor in terms of performances. We turned it around and had good games, but if you look at our Test match record, we've played four matches and haven't batted a full day.' That would change in Perth, but as was the case in Melbourne it would again be Ambrose, rather than their batsmen, who changed the course of the game for them.

At the WACA, Lara took up where he had left off in the second innings in Adelaide, but this time he showed even more application and went on to score a century. Perhaps the high temperatures had thawed him out of hibernation. Perth provides a different sort of heat to any other cricket-playing city in the world. It gets very hot, but it's a dry heat and you don't sweat much. In places such as India it's more uncomfortable because, while it may not be quite as hot as Perth, there's almost 100 per cent humidity and the air is so thick you can hardly breathe. But with a difficult wicket and a battery of top-class speedsters operating, that first day in Perth was as uncomfortable as anything I've experienced.

On that first morning, I was in with the score at 2–7 and ready to face the music. I can only feel for those poor tormented souls who had to face the likes of Lillee and Thomson in the days before helmets. The only good thing about batting against the Windies during a Perth heatwave is that it's just as hot for the bowlers, and they have to expend more energy charging in. Against Ambrose that day, we knew he was not going to last very long at top pace, so our tactics were to see him off and then try and make some runs from the other guys. My 79 in that first innings only prolonged the agony for everyone, but it was one of my better Test digs.

As Simon Hughes wrote: 'Lump two teams of loping, accurate fast bowlers together on a strip of fractured concrete and an early finish is inevitable, especially with Australia having already won the series.'

With Walsh off the field after just nine overs on the first day with a hamstring injury, stand-in skipper Lara used Ambrose and Bishop in one-over spells into the breeze late in the day. These were good tactics, one over and then a 10-minute rest before coming on again. Those sort of tactics haven't been used too much in international cricket, but they made a lot of sense. And they were very effective. Showing little or no effect of the thigh problem that kept him sidelined in Adelaide, Ambrose revelled in the heat.

In two previous Tests on that wicket he had taken 17 wickets and after less than one day of his third match in Perth he had another 5–43. Humiliated so many times earlier in the series, Ambrose got his revenge. He came out onto the pitch for the first morning waving goodbye to the Aussie fans, but he might as well have been waving goodbye to the Australian batsmen. It was a disappointment for us to end our series against the West Indies in defeat, but the series had already been wrapped up so there weren't too many tears.

Early in the series, the lack of hunger from the West Indian team, their shoddiness in the field and their indiscipline with the bat had cost them dearly. Combine those drawbacks with the fact that man for man we had a slightly better side and it's no wonder they suffered in the lead-up to Perth. In the first four Tests of the series we were a much more determined bunch than them. They had internal problems and in-fighting and Lara's storming into our

THE FIFTH TEST—THE WACA

change-room in Sydney highlighted the disharmony among their ranks.

In the first two Tests the West Indian fielding let them down and the critics said it looked as though Ambrose wasn't trying in the field. I don't think we'll ever see Australian players show that sort of disinterest in the game. Discipline was certainly not the best feature of the West Indians in 1996–97; and in the situations where they did well, it was their natural ability more than anything that carried it off. But while they lacked discipline on the tour, the West Indians are proud people. They don't like losing at any time and with the series gone we knew they would come back at us hard and fast in Perth. Fast being the operative word.

Ambrose's first delivery of the Test was a no-ball, but only three balls later he had Matt Hayden, caught by Lara in the slips for nought. Seven runs later, Mark Taylor was run out after Shivnarine Chanderpaul showed the sort of fielding the West Indians could have been displaying throughout the series. And in another rare moment, Greg Blewett was caught by Courtney Browne off Phil Simmons in one of the few bright spots Phil had on tour.

Michael Bevan and I put on 120 but it wasn't enough to save the game. I was on 36 when I tried to hook one off Curtly and instead copped it right in the grille of my helmet. It was the weirdest thing. Believe it or not I didn't feel a thing. I thought there must be some damage somewhere and I was waiting for the shock to wear off and the pain to hit. But not a thing. I guess it shows you just how good the helmets are these days.

I managed to outlast Ambrose and Bishop for two sessions and lofted Carl Hooper for six, but Curtly got me, caught by Sherwin

Campbell at third slip in his first over after tea. Shortly afterwards, he bowled another over that claimed Ian Healy and Paul Reiffel with consecutive deliveries.

Bishop, who looked like he was ready to drop in the afternoon sun and at one time was vomiting, somehow managed to hold himself together and find the strength to mop up the tail, getting Andy Bichel and Glenn McGrath with two bouncers. For the second successive time, Bevvo was left stranded in the 80s. We were all out for 243 and Ambrose came off as he had come onto the field, waving to the fans.

Day 2, and Reiffel and McGrath had the Windies at 2–43, but then Lara, with some stubborn and at times scratchy back-up from young Robert Samuels, put together the match-winning partnership, adding 208 runs and treading on plenty of our toes in the process. Lara had introduced golf star Ernie Els to the Windies players after the first day's play and he continued the risky drives, slices, hooks and cuts that had characterised his tour. Despite three slips and three gullies and the close attention of Glenn McGrath, Lara hit his first Test century since blasting Devon Malcolm and Angus Fraser at the Oval 18 months earlier. It was about time.

When Lara edged Warne's top-spinner to Ian Healy, Warney had picked up his 229th Test wicket, taking him past Ray Lindwall to become Australia's fifth highest Test wicket-taker. That's some achievement for a bloke who has been on the Test scene only a few short years.

Robert Samuels had hit only 51 of the 208-run stand with Lara, but he was to figure much more prominently in the game as Lara tried to ignite a sledging row. Ignoring the policy of what is said on the field stays on the field, Lara used the press conference after

THE FIFTH TEST—THE WACA

his century to vent his spleen on the Australians, saying we had sledged Samuels unmercifully.

'Australia have won the series and congratulations to them, but they seem to be rubbing it in at this point in time,' Lara said. 'With a youngster who is trying his best and whose Test future is in a bit of a doubt and he's working as hard as possible, I was a bit disappointed with the Australian approach to him.' Lara said umpires Darrell Hair and Peter Willey intervened and 'tried to calm things down'.

Lara was on a roll. 'I didn't think it was necessary to react in such a way, especially after you've won a series,' Lara stated. 'They were talking about losers and stuff like that and it wasn't necessary.' Lara also had a warning for the Australians. 'We're going to bounce back,' he said. 'We've got them in two years' time [in the Caribbean] and, I promise you, we'll not be losing.'

Lara acknowledged that the West Indies were sometimes involved in 'confrontations' but added 'when there is an all-day sledging and stuff like that of one particular player, it's unnecessary. When I asked one of the guys to cool out, he said he wouldn't say anything to me but only to "that loser" up there.'

The only way I can think to explain Lara's outburst is that he craves being the centre of attention so much that he is prepared to make an incident out of anything. It seemed a terribly childish thing to do. To me, the whole thing was none of Lara's business really. Robert Samuels is a big boy and I didn't hear him complaining too much. He wasn't worried about it. The worst things being said were things such as 'You think you're good—it's taken you four hours to hit one in the middle. You're an ordinary player.' That sort of thing. There was certainly nothing personal.

It was nothing out of the ordinary. After the match, Mark Taylor said Lara was as great a provocateur as Sri Lanka's Mr Controversy, Arjuna Ranatunga. I'd go along with that.

It always seems Lara is causing trouble when there is no need. I'm sure when he looks back on his career in a few years, he will wish he had reacted differently to certain situations, especially his blow-up over Ian Healy in Sydney. Lara sometimes puts himself before the game, making himself bigger than the game, which he most definitely isn't. Over the years he's had run-ins with Andy Roberts, the Windies' physio and other players. I think he'd do a lot better if he just stuck to his batting and kept his trap shut. He showed no class at all in his press conference. However, at the crease in this match, he showed plenty. By the end of Day 2, with his significant contribution, the Windies had managed 7–353; their highest total against Australia for four years and the first time they'd batted for a day in the series.

On the third morning Lara acted as a runner for Walsh. The fact that Walsh needed a runner and then came out and bowled 20 consecutive overs against us, was just another bizarre occurrence in a bizarre match. I guess Walsh was just protecting his hamstring. He probably thought he was okay to just bat and was worried that he'd risk aggravating the injury by running. I think he was probably planning to take his bowling over by over in our second innings and in the end he managed to get through an awful lot of hard work. The Windies went on to make 384 despite a five-wicket haul from Paul Reiffel.

We lined up for our second innings at 141 runs in arrears and with Ambrose stoking up the boiler for a fiery farewell, we knew we were in for another hot time in the middle. Tubby Taylor was caught behind for one and Greg Blewett fell for nought after copping a ball that shot along the ground like one of Ricky Ponting's greyhounds after the lure. With Ambrose hobbling, it was left to Walsh to lope in over after over, picking up 5–74 off his 20 overs.

When Curtly came back, he bowled nine no-balls in his last over as he tried attacking from around the wicket. Bishop finally snared Warney and we were all out for 194. Campbell and Samuels then put on 56 without loss for a victory by 10 wickets inside three days. Curtly took Man-of-the-Match honours for his ferocity in the first innings, but Walsh could easily have won the same for his big-hearted bowling in the second.

I think it will be a long time before the Windies come up with a fast bowler as good as those two and although newcomer Franklyn Rose has been receiving some big wraps of late, he has some enormous boots to fill. Tubby acknowledged the greatness of the Windies pacemen as he cradled the Frank Worrell trophy. 'Well done, you've been fantastic bowlers,' Tubby said at the presentation, 'but speaking personally I'm glad not to be seeing you again.'

And so say all of us.

Australia v. West Indies

This is my report card on the performance of all players involved in the Australia v. West Indies Test series of 1996–97.

AUSTRALIA

MARK TAYLOR
5 TESTS   153 RUNS AT 17.00 (AV.)   HIGHEST SCORE: 43

A great triumph as captain, but a disappointing series as an opening bat on some tough batting tracks against quality bowling. Still, there is not a more inspiring or dignified leader in the game.

MATTHEW ELLIOTT
2 TESTS   128 RUNS AT 42.66   HS: 78 NOT OUT

Really showed great promise as an opening batsman, with a great technique and a variety of shots. His running between wickets needed some work!

MATTHEW HAYDEN
3 TESTS 177 RUNS AT 35.40 HS: 125

His century in Adelaide was a fitting reward for a bloke who has dominated first-class attacks for years without the rewards at the highest level. He also top scored in the Perth second innings to show he can make the next step from first-class cricket to Test level.

MARK WAUGH
5 TESTS 370 RUNS AT 41.11 HS: 82
0 WICKETS FOR 31

I was reasonably happy with my form, but disappointed that I didn't turn a couple of the half-centuries into three figures, especially in Adelaide where the conditions were ideal for a big score.

GREG BLEWETT
4 TESTS 301 RUNS AT 50.16 HS: 99
1 WICKET AT 64.00 BEST: 1–13

A welcome return to the Test scene. He quickly demonstrated the flair and daring that would flourish even more in South Africa. A player of real class.

STEPHEN WAUGH
4 TESTS 188 RUNS AT 31.33 HS: 66
1 WICKET AT 63.00 BEST: 1–15

Had a quiet series by his usual high standards, but his 66 in Brisbane helped us establish a 1–0 lead over the Windies and put the pressure on the visitors. Stephen was quickly back to form in South Africa.

MICHAEL BEVAN
4 TESTS 275 RUNS AT 55.00 HS: 87 NOT OUT
15 WICKETS AT 17.66 BEST 6–82

A tremendous all-round performance in a series that saw Bevvo emerge as one of the world's most dangerous spin bowlers. He destroyed the Windies with a 10-wicket performance in Adelaide and was twice left stranded in the 80s when Australia were all out. He looked a more confident Test player by the end of the series.

RICKY PONTING
2 TESTS 110 RUNS AT 27.50 HS: 88
1 WICKET FOR NO RUNS

Ricky wasn't overly blessed with opportunities. He made 88 in Brisbane, but was dropped from the team before Melbourne. He remains one of the most exciting players in the game and I was sure he'd bounce back in the baggy green cap. How about those bowling figures?

JUSTIN LANGER
2 TESTS 31 RUNS AT 10.33 HS: 19

Unfortunately, he batted on a testing wicket in Melbourne where luck was against him, being run out and bowled by a pull shot onto his stumps. Missed out in Adelaide, but has plenty of guts and determination in his favour.

IAN HEALY
5 TESTS 356 RUNS AT 59.33 HS: 161 NOT OUT
15 CATCHES

What's a better superlative than magnificent? Stupendous? Fantastic? Unsurpassable?

Ian Healy proved his class as a batsman, wicket-keeper and fighter. His 161 in Brisbane set the tone for the series and just about broke the sore backs of the Windies bowlers. His work behind the stumps was superb and with many critics calling for him to be replaced by Adam Gilchrist he showed the heart of Evander Holyfield. At one stage his batting average was something like 250 for the series. Enough said.

SHANE WARNE
5 TESTS 128 RUNS AT 18.28 HS: 30
22 WICKETS AT 27.00 BEST: 4–95

These days Warney is expected to wreck every team he plays, and although he didn't devastate the Windies, he still took heaps of wickets. He averaged more than four a match and combined magnificently with Bevvo for a lethal combination in Adelaide.

GLENN MCGRATH
5 TESTS 32 RUNS AT 6.40 HS: 24
26 WICKETS AT 17.42 BEST: 5–50

Man of the Series. He bowled with speed, accuracy and determination all series, taking 5–50 in Adelaide and never giving the West Indies a break in the five Tests, but his budding career as a batting saviour was short-lived after his 24 in Sydney.

PAUL REIFFEL
3 TESTS 44 RUNS AT 7.33 HS: 20
12 WICKETS AT 25.41 BEST: 5–73

When he was fit he bowled very well, especially in Perth. A great line and length. Unfortunately, he suffered from injuries throughout the series; injuries that would plague him in South

Psychologically we were at a low ebb as we geared up to meet the West Indies in a five Test series at home. We quickly forgot the nightmare of India though, because we had new horrors to contend with such as facing Walsh and Ambrose at top pace on a lively wicket in the First Test at the Gabba *(above)*.

Shane Warne appeals during the first Test *(below)*.

Curtly Ambrose' farewell series in Australia – he certainly went out in style. No one shed a tear over his departure. We were just glad we wouldn't see him again on fast Australian wickets.

After the fifth Test, Australia v West Indies, in Perth. Curtly Ambrose took Man-of-the-Match honours *(above)* for his ferocity in the first innings. Tubby acknowledged the greatness of the Windies pacemen as he held the Frank Worrell trophy aloft *(below)*.

Stephen asking South African umpire, Cyril Mitchley for some hints about the South African bowlers.

Stephen and Blewie walk off the field after their match winning partnership in the 1st Test in Johannesburg.

Congratulating Stephen during the 2nd One Day at Port Elizabeth.

Africa. His best game was in Perth with five wickets, but his bowling performance could not compensate for our small totals.

JASON GILLESPIE
2 TESTS 22 RUNS AT 22.00 HS: 16 NOT OUT
2 WICKETS AT 47.00

Broke down after just three overs in Melbourne, but bowled as fast as anyone in the world. Though we didn't get to see much of him, we saw enough to know that he could be anything in Test cricket, if he remained injury free. A fast whippy action, a menacing appearance and plenty of Devil in him makes Dizzy a handful for any batting side.

MICHAEL KASPROWICZ
2 TESTS 27 RUNS AT 13.50 HS: 21
0 WICKETS FOR 126

A frustrating series for him, going wicketless before his home crowd at the Gabba and again at Sydney. He bowled much better than the statistics showed and was very unlucky not to have picked up at least a couple of scalps on debut.

ANDREW BICHEL
2 TESTS 40 RUNS AT 13.33 HS: 18
1 WICKET AT 143.00 BEST 1–31

Didn't get a swag of wickets in limited appearances, but he is a tough, honest campaigner. He is a genuine swing bowler who will bowl all day for you.

WEST INDIES

SHERWIN CAMPBELL
5 TESTS 291 RUNS AT 32.33 HS: 113

Started the series with a century in Brisbane in what was a lost cause for the Windies. He's a good player, without looking anything great. His footwork wasn't terrific, but the little Barbadian's resistance in Brisbane kept us in the field right to the end.

ROBERT SAMUELS
4 TESTS 231 RUNS AT 33.00 HS: 76

He scored 76 in Perth, but overall did nothing exceptional on the tour and seemed to be a fairly limited batsman. His innings in Perth was a marathon effort, but he never really looked comfortable out there.

ADRIAN GRIFFITH
1 TEST 14 RUNS AT 7.00 HS: 13

The figures reflect his series. He showed very little at all. In fact he looked like a club standard cricketer. That's harsh, but fair.

BRIAN LARA
5 TESTS 296 RUNS AT 32.88 HS: 132

I said a year before the series that Lara and Sachin Tendulkar were the best batsmen in the world, but Stephen has overtaken them both. Obviously, Lara is a match-winning player who holds the world record for highest first-class and Test scores.

Lately though, he has shown that he is always a chance of getting out because he is always keen to have a go and play his shots. When the Windies really needed him to perform early in the Test series against us, he was averaging 12 and he only came good when the series was lost. Despite his shortcomings he is always dangerous and can change a game very quickly.

SHIVNARINE CHANDERPAUL
5 TESTS   344 RUNS AT 38.22   HS: 82
1 WICKET FOR 2 RUNS

He was the best of the Windies batsmen on tour and the hardest of their players to get out. He has an unusual, but effective, technique. He plays back and across all the time and watches the ball very closely and tends to play late. But he batted with a lot of flair and was prepared to take his time and build his innings. Never got to three figures against us, but showed a lot of class trying.

CARL HOOPER
5 TESTS   362 RUNS AT 45.25   HS: 102
3 WICKETS AT 105.66   BEST: 2–86

At times he looked brilliant and at times ordinary. An immensely gifted player who doesn't always deliver when he's expected to. On his day he's a great hitter and an exciting player to watch.

JIMMY ADAMS
5 TESTS   140 RUNS AT 20.00 HS: 74 NOT OUT
1 WICKET FOR 59   BEST 1–11

Once rated the world's best batsman, he never seems to do any good against us. He's a very gutsy player who hangs in there without ever looking like the sort of batsman who'll rip an attack to pieces.

COURTNEY BROWNE
3 TESTS 49 RUNS AT 12.25 HS: 25 NOT OUT
15 CATCHES

He was far too erratic for a Test wicket-keeper and his batting wasn't much good. Tended to drop the regulation catches but took the hard ones. As they say, there are no points for looking pretty.

JUNIOR MURRAY
2 TESTS 112 RUNS AT 37.33 HS: 53
4 CATCHES, 1 STUMPING

Murray batted with a great deal of aggression, but like Browne, his keeping was always unpredictable and often substandard for Test matches. He delighted the fans at the MCG with his eagerness to swing the bat, but too many times it was hit and miss.

IAN BISHOP
5 TESTS 86 RUNS AT 10.75 HS: 48
20 WICKETS AT 25.50 BEST: 3–49

Bishop has lost pace and control from his early days. I remember him as a truly devastating bowler early in his career. Even though injuries have slowed him down, he is still quite dangerous on his day and a great third bowler for any side. He bowled extremely well in the first couple of Tests and was always a worry.

KENNY BENJAMIN
3 TESTS 31 RUNS AT 6.20 HS: 11
9 WICKETS AT 40.22 BEST: 3–34

He's a shade or two below Ambrose and Walsh, but still a lively bowler. I have flashbacks from the monster headache his bouncer gave me in Brisbane. He hits the seam a lot and the ball tends to hurry off the wicket more than you expect. The Windies suffered when he was eventually ruled out of the last two Tests with injury.

COURTNEY WALSH
5 TESTS   31 RUNS AT 7.75 HS: 18
19 WICKETS AT 31.15 BEST: 5–74

Walsh bowled with real pace on occasions, but usually bowled a little within himself. With his whippy action, great bouncer, tremendous control and high work ethic he was always a difficult opponent. As a skipper, he was fairly defensive throughout—never giving away easy runs. He was a lion-hearted player who had the respect of his team and would bend his back all day.

CURTLY AMBROSE
4 TESTS   39 RUNS AT 6.50   HS: 15
19 WICKETS AT 23.36 BEST 5–43

A Test match winner on two occasions, he showed in Melbourne and Perth the kind of speed, accuracy and class that has made him one of the true legends of cricket with more than 300 Test victims. His fielding was poor at times and occasionally he looked very lazy when things weren't going his way. But as soon as he saw an opening in our armour he stuck in the knife.

PHIL SIMMONS
1 TEST   0 RUNS
1 WICKET AT 67.00   BEST 1–58

For all the good Simmons did in his lone Test, he might as well have stayed home. He came out to play in Perth and didn't score a run. But the truth is that Simmons isn't a bad player. He can bat, bowl and field, but he just doesn't seem to be able to show his true ability in Test matches when the pressure is on.

PATTERSON THOMPSON
1 TEST 16 RUNS AT 16.00 HS: 10 NOT OUT
1 WICKET AT 80.00

Could be quite pacey when he wanted, but played with a total lack of discipline in Adelaide. He looked like a Z-grade cricketer in his approach to the game and was only given half the work of his fellow bowlers in that match.

CAMERON CUFFY
1 TEST 5 RUNS AT 5.00 HS: 3 NOT OUT
2 WICKETS AT 58.00 BEST: 2–116

Cuffy bowled steadily and with fair pace, but he was no Ambrose or Walsh. He didn't do a lot wrong, but he never looked likely to threaten us like their big guns.

The Art of Touring

'I think I'd end up in Callan Park lunatic asylum playing cricket day after day, and that one-day rubbish.'

FORMER TEST BATSMAN ARTHUR MORRIS

On 17 March 1996 at Gaddafi Stadium in Lahore, Sri Lanka gave us a lesson in one-day cricket. And the whole world for that matter.

The explosive opening batting from a side once considered the minnows of the game propelled Sri Lanka out of nowhere to become major players on the world cricket stage. They revolutionised one-day cricket with their pinch hitting and their relentless scoring of boundaries in the first 15 overs. The sensational starts of their two openers Jayasuriya and Kaluwitharana so often laid a platform that other teams just couldn't overcome.

Of course, there is a difference in playing one-day cricket in Australia and on the subcontinent. In India, Pakistan and Sri Lanka, you can bat with a degree of recklessness not possible in Australia. The wickets over there are flat and the grounds small and fast and you can tee off there from the first ball. I can guarantee no batsman playing on bouncy Australian wickets would be taking apart bowlers such as Curtly Ambrose and Wasim Akram in the first few overs of a one-day match.

Sri Lanka did exceptionally well in the World Cup, showing the way with their dynamite batting and fast athletic fielding. It was certainly a letdown for us to have gone so far in the World Cup and then to have lost to Sri Lanka in the final. We had played some outstanding cricket to get there, having whipped the Kiwis and the West Indians in a couple of thrillers. But what was an even bigger disappointment for us was not making the Carlton and United finals series back home, which Pakistan eventually took in fairly one-sided fashion against the West Indies.

It was the first time in 17 years that we had not made the final of the international one-day series at home and we had no-one to blame but ourselves. We were eventually eliminated against the Windies in Perth on January 12 in a crucial match sandwiched between the Melbourne and Adelaide Tests. The Windies pulled off a thrilling four-wicket win after Brian Lara hit 90 in 110 balls to steer them home with four deliveries to spare. We thought we had a great chance after I hit 92 out of 267, despite hurting my hamstring, but Lara and Robert Samuels hit 86 between them off only 51 balls and it was goodnight.

Pakistan virtually won the series by default. We played below par and probably threw away three or four games. The Windies were certainly not the same athletic, committed side they had been on previous tours. Pakistan won the series largely through their bowling with the off-spin of Saqlain and the wily pace of Akram. Their bowling attack was their backbone. I really believe that if we had played anywhere near our best cricket we could not only have made the final, but taken out the trophy.

There is so much one-day cricket these days that Australia really has to start treating the 50-over game with the same importance it gives to Test matches. There are more and more countries being accepted into the international fold. In recent years Zimbabwe, South Africa and Sri Lanka have all been added to the international schedule. The countries on the subcontinent are always looking to host a one-day series. Everyone is looking to make money for their national body and the boards often play off each other. It's a case of 'we'll give you a series there if you come over for a series here'.

There's always the chance of players burning out from simply playing too much and the players are the last people a lot of the cricket boards are thinking about. I guess we are professional cricketers and if you have a normal job you work most of the year so we just have to accept the fact that as cricketers we have to play a lot more than we have previously.

The major problem from the immense workload on players these days is the injuries. You get players going out there wanting to keep their place and afraid that if they give it up for a match or two, someone will cement it for himself. So you get players going out onto the field with niggles and below their best and it means the standard of cricket suffers and the best players won't always be on show.

I love the life of a touring cricketer, but there are still things that really annoy me. Like the one-off Test we had to play in India and the uncomfortable situation in which we are still made to share rooms a lot of the time on tour. All these little things add up, but in the end we must concentrate on playing and let the newly formed ACA (players' association) handle these things for us.

Shane Warne recently said in an interview that the bloke he most hated sharing a room with was me because I'm so untidy. Obviously he had me mixed up with Stephen. Sharing rooms does take a lot of compromise between roomies though. In the Tests we get a room to ourselves, but for the other games it's often a fight over who gets the bed by the window and who has to put the light out. Whenever we get into our shared rooms, the housemaids always seem to have the beds hard up against each other. Don't ask me why. They must think we're all terribly close. Something to do with male bonding. Whatever. The first job is to push the beds as far apart as possible and make sure we all have our personal space. There's a lot of give and take.

Michael Bevan, for instance, is a very light sleeper and it's tough if he's sharing with a bloke who likes watching TV, or comes back to the hotel a bit later or is doing interviews or has phone calls home to make.

The people who aren't playing—the scorer, the physio, the fitness trainer and manager—all get their own rooms. As far as I'm concerned, the players are at least as important and I think it's something that may change in the future. But we have a great squad of players these days and generally we cope well with each other's bad and good habits.

Enter South Africa

'They really want to murder us. If they do, they will see themselves as world champions back to where they were in 1970.'

FORMER AUSTRALIAN FAST BOWLER AND NOW EASTERN PROVINCE COACH JEFF HAMMOND, ON THE EVE OF AUSTRALIA'S TEST SERIES IN SOUTH AFRICA

It's the faces I'll always remember. Happy faces, white teeth and shining eyes full of life and hope. Two thousand or more kids in a crowd of 3000 had come to the Soweto Cricket Oval to see the Australian team beat a Transvaal Invitation XI on 25 February. The venue was a converted rubbish dump in one of the poorest cities on earth. It was the least competitive match we played all tour, but it may have been the most important. It was a game of cricket in which it didn't matter if we won or lost, only that we played the game.

To get an idea of what life is like in Soweto you must look at the deaths. Only a week before we played there a man who had been accused of killing three children was caught by vigilantes, shot, doused with petrol and set alight with a burning car tyre. This was nothing out of the ordinary in a city that must have more barbed wire and machine guns than any other on the globe. But when the

Aussie cricket team played there, the smiles on the faces of these kids pushed all the hardships behind.

Materially these youngsters might have nothing. The comforts of life that young people back home in Australia take for granted are a world away for the poorest black children in South Africa's poorest city. But no amount of money could buy the joy these kids showed when the Aussies hit their home town. The kids had been bussed in to make a crowd and, even though most of them probably didn't know the difference between a silly mid-on and a smart cover drive, they had a ball.

Ten years ago the Soweto Cricket Oval was a rubbish dump where the only signs of life were the roaches and stray dogs picking over scraps missed by hungry kids fossicking among the refuse. It was smack bang in the middle of a desperately overcrowded, ramshackle city that had become a symbol to the world of apartheid—South Africa's infamous policy of racial segregation. It was a city teeming with crime, violence and poverty.

Ten years later, the crime, violence and poverty are still there and the sprawling ramshackle city, its tumble-down houses of corrugated iron and cardboard and its million residents are still reminders of South Africa's apartheid legacy. Barbed wire surrounds the oval, security forces there for the match carried machine guns and a couple of kids watched the action from the top of an armoured police car, which looked a lot like an army tank. Not the sort of thing you see every day at the SCG.

In 10 years, however, the Soweto Cricket Oval has become good enough to host a first-class match, and the beaming kids who kept the Aussie players signing autographs all day are symbols of the new South Africa, the new confidence and hope among the black community. We did our best to make it a match the kids in the crowd and the young hopefuls in the Transvaal XI will never forget. South African cricket chief Ali Bacher dreams of one day seeing kids from the poor black townships playing for their country. And from what we saw in Soweto and other cricket centres such as the Dan Qeqe Stadium in Zwide, there's no reason why in a few years their national team won't be fielding black players. The enthusiasm and the potential is certainly there.

Three years ago the Aussie team held a coaching clinic at Soweto, next door to the present oval. In those days the cricket ground was just a couple of concrete pitches and a rough outfield. But with $400,000 from sponsorships, the United Cricket Board of South Africa made it something special. Certainly I'll never forget playing there. School kids in a brass band must have struck up 'Waltzing Matilda' about 20 times, but no-one got sick of it.

The match was played in terrific spirit with a real festival atmosphere, just three days before the serious combat of the First Test at the Wanderers. Despite the good nature of the game at Soweto, the Transvaal boys showed plenty of fight. Geoffrey Toyana is one Soweto cricketer they all say has a big future, even though he only made three against us. Another player named Johnson Mafa bowled with plenty of heart at first change and caught me out first ball. Solomon Ndima is a plucky little bloke who hit us around for 35.

We had the Transvaal lads at 5–29, but put the brakes on and let them back into the game, knocking back a couple of certain l.b.w. appeals to Michael Bevan and Jason Gillespie. The local cricketers chased and skidded all over the place to save every run they could even when our victory was a foregone conclusion. More importantly, those players made further advances toward cricket in South Africa becoming a truly multi-racial sport. Ali Bacher told us that about 300 concrete pitches had already been laid in the black townships over the previous 18 months and that eventually there'll be a thousand. 'It's about life, giving opportunity and race relations,' he said. The Soweto match brought some light relief in a series which was filled with pressure.

The World Championship of Cricket; that's how the media built up the tour and obviously the hype affected everyone. While I reckon Pakistan might have something to say about a world championship that didn't feature them, we weren't complaining about the huge publicity campaign in South Africa. Coming off the series against the West Indies, we looked toward our trip across the Indian Ocean as another formidable challenge, knowing we were up against tenacious batsmen, great fast bowlers, committed fieldsmen and parochial crowds.

However, we've thought for a long time that South Africa were a little suspect under pressure and the more expectations heaped upon Hansie Cronje and his blokes, the happier we were. As an example, South Africa had built an incredible record of 33 one-day victories in their past 38 internationals going into our series. They'd just put together seven wins on the trot against India. But in the big events like the World Cup, they were bundled out in the quarter-finals and looked a little ordinary. We were hopeful that they'd feel the same heat from us when we touched down there.

The trip over had been longer than usual. For our previous tour Qantas had provided the airfares and we had flown straight from Perth for 10 hours to Johannesburg. For this tour, Cathay Pacific were our sponsors and we travelled to South Africa via Hong

Kong, which is not exactly the shortest distance from A to B. It made the trip a day longer, but it did give us a chance to have a drink together that night in a fabulous city and do a bit of duty-free shopping. So no-one was complaining.

What we were complaining about at the start of the tour was the new fitness regime put together by Steve Smith, our personal trainer on tour. The game of cricket has certainly changed immensely over the 12 years I've been playing at first-class level. Steve's a great bloke and an ex-Navy man who coached Geoff Marsh's footy team in WA. He's covered in tattoos and looks as tough as his training methods. He worked with a few of the West Coast Eagles on their personal fitness and runs a gym in Perth. He knows what he's doing, but believe me, this new emphasis on training took a lot of getting used to.

In years gone by, cricketers on long overseas trips were infamous for setting beer consumption records. The empty cans would pile up like run aggregates. These days, young blokes like Matt Hayden and Greg Blewett spend every spare minute in the gym. For the guys over 30 like me, who have been used to a more relaxed approach, fitness regimes are about as welcome as wake-up calls, but they tell me it's good for you. I guess I'll have to take their word for it.

On days when I don't have much to do, I like to stay in bed till nine or ten o'clock. I like my sleep. But on tour we're generally out of bed at seven. I'm not an early morning person at the best of times, but on this tour Steve Smith had us up early for morning walks, doing boxing training and heading to the gym. Everyone had their own personal programs. Some blokes were even running home from games.

In the late 1990s, cricket is more scientific than ever, even down to the fact that South Africa's coach, Bob Woolmer, has taken to computers to gain an edge. While we have started using videos at team meetings to analyse the weaknesses of opposition batsmen and bowlers, Woolmer has brought even more advanced ideas to South Africa. A former Test batsman and World Series Cricket veteran, he had great success as a coach at Warwickshire a few years back. He now records every ball of every match South Africa plays on his laptop computer, working out scoring patterns and bowling trends. Woolmer has placed a big emphasis on stacking the South African team with all-rounders, fast bowlers like Lance Klusener and Shaun Pollock, who can really bat, and batsmen like Hansie Cronje and Jacques Kallis, who are handy with the ball. This was obviously a tour that meant a great deal to South African cricket.

The importance of the series and of sport's role in changing the social climate in South Africa was rammed home to us at a welcoming dinner in Jo'burg two days after we touched down. Professor Kader Asmal, South Africa's Minister for Forestry and Water Affairs in the Mandela government, is a former school teacher and barrister and founder of the British Anti-Apartheid Movement in London. He was forced to live in exile from his country until 1990. He pointed out that as Forestry and Water Affairs Minister he had a tremendous affinity with cricket, given the impact of willow and rain on the game. Normally, welcoming speeches for cricket tours are pretty boring, but Professor Asmal spoke with power and passion, recalling the day as a 12-year-old boy when he was locked in the 'blacks only' enclosure at Durban, watching Lindsay Hassett's Australians win a thrilling Test match on the 1949–50 tour.

In those days the South African cricket team was a symbol of white oppression to the blacks and Professor Asmal brought a tear to a few eyes and nervous shuffles from some of the older white South African officials when he told the audience how he barracked wildly for the Aussies on that day. No-one made a sound as he recalled how he raced out onto the field and tried to lift Neil Harvey onto his shoulders after a memorable innings of 151 not out. Thankfully for everyone in South Africa, apartheid is gone. But the legacy of poverty, hate and suspicion lingers.

The crime in places like Johannesburg is worse than ever. Our first tour to South Africa, in 1994, was Australia's first visit to the republic in 24 years and it rammed home to us that such tours are fraught with danger. Both on and off the field. For our first visit we had a team of bodyguards including a 190-centimetre, raw-boned boxer named Pierre Coetzer, who was once rated a top contender for Mike Tyson's title in the early 1990s and who slugged it out with such big names as George Foreman, Riddick Bowe and Frank Bruno. Pierre looked ferocious, with a moustache nearly as wide as his XXXL shoulders and hands like buckets. Though he was never required to use his huge fists on our behalf, his presence reinforced the fact that life in South Africa has plenty of perils.

For our tour in 1997, we had two armed guards with us most of the way. In places like Jo'burg—crime capital of the world—there were ever-present signs of violence and fear. There's a fortress mentality in the more expensive areas with electronic gates to all the palatial homes and barbed wire atop the high fences. The police carry machine guns and look ready to use them. The crime statistics make grim reading. It's said that every year in

South Africa there are 40,000 murders. More than 100 a day.

At the Holiday Inn in Johannesburg at the end of the Third Test, some of the Foxtel commentary team were woken by gunfire as bandits killed one hotel staff member and riddled a wall with bullets. The killing didn't even make the papers, violent crime being so common. The Australian High Commission in Pretoria provided the team with what was called a 'survival guide'—a two-page list of guidelines to help us avoid dangerous situations.

While our previous tour had been incident free, the fact we had never seen any trouble didn't mean it wasn't out there. Staying in good hotels and travelling together meant we were safer than the average bloke on the street. While most cities are the focal point for any tourist, on this trip we weren't taking any chances. Wives and girlfriends are often by themselves for long periods on a cricket tour and South Africa is not the kind of place where you would feel safe leaving them alone.

The High Commissioner came to see us at the start of the tour and gave us specific warnings. 'Stay well clear of Jo'burg's central area and be very cautious in the beachfront regions of Durban,' he told us. 'Never go out on foot alone and never go out on foot at night, even in groups. Since car-jackings are common and the murder rate is sky high, be ready to take evasive action if approached by strangers at traffic lights.' There was even a directive that if our car was hijacked we should just get out straight away, leaving wallets and valuables.

No-one is immune from crime in South Africa. Their first black Olympic gold medallist, Josiah Thugawane, the marathon runner, has been car-jacked twice. When he won the Atlanta Olympic marathon he still bore a scar from a robber's bullet that grazed his face. He says, seriously, that he'll defend his title in Sydney in 2000, if he's still alive. The climate of fear is unnerving to say the least and thankfully there were no incidents to test out the High Commissioner's survival theories.

But there was a lighter side. When former Test dasher and now commentator David Hookes had his wallet swiped from his hotel in Durban, the thief racked up $13,000 on Hookesy's credit card in two days before he was caught. 'I'm actually dirty they caught him,' Hookesy said, straight-faced. 'The fact he spent $13,000 in two days is nothing to what my wife Robyn will do with the new card. She has a black belt in shopping. She shops off scratch.'

While we were prepared for anything on the streets of South Africa, we were also prepared for a torrid time on the field. Even our first training session of the tour saw some of the side hit the deck as a blast like cannon fire rocked the Wanderers ground in Jo'burg. Lightning can strike terror into the bravest of souls and we didn't need a second invitation from Tubby to get on the team bus and get out of there.

Perhaps it was an omen of some rough days ahead, but a few days later in our first match on tour, we were given little resistance against the Oppenheimer Invitational XI at Randjesfontein. We played on the private cricket ground of mining bigwig Nicky Oppenheimer beneath picturesque rolling hills on the outskirts of Johannesburg. Nicky loves his cricket and has built one of the most beautiful grounds I've ever seen, some 1600 metres above sea level. It's complete with the best fine couch grass you can get and a ring of grand cypress trees on the boundary.

The Oppenheimer match has been a feature for touring teams since South Africa's re-introduction to the Test scene and Nicky gets to host it by coughing up about $30,000 plus proceeds from the match to the United Cricket Board of South Africa's development fund. The donation always assured Nicky a place in his own side against some of the best cricketers in the world, despite his rather modest talents. This year Nicky's place was taken by his son Jonathon, an Oxford blue. He's no great player either, but he did prance around for a while like a good sort. I sat the game out and Tubby batted at four, his form slump continuing as he was out for 18.

In the end we made 6–284 and got them out for 265, with South African Test candidate Neil McKenzie making 133. The team also included a promising black fast bowler named Makhaya Ntini, who has represented South Africa in the under-19s and who seems to be one of Ali Bacher's big hopes for township cricketers. Jason Gillespie took 2–33 with all-out aggression and that whippy action.

He was again in the hunt in Australia's next match against Western Province at Newlands in the beautiful city of Cape Town. Again my role in the side was as a spectator. Dizzy generated pace and Andy Bichel bowled really well to collect five wickets. Bevvo claimed three in a marathon effort and Western skipper John Commins said he was going to be a 'real force'. He was right about that.

The most pleasing aspect of the Western Province match for us was Tubby's long-awaited return to form. He played well against an attack that featured internationals Brian McMillan, Brett Schultz, Craig Matthews and Meyrick Pringle, and in the end hit 85. It was his best first-class score since making 96 in the Perth Test against Sri Lanka 14 months earlier. After the match, he told the media: 'Obviously I was worried about my form. I don't like it being seen as the side carrying me. I've always believed the captain has to make some runs and I've always wanted to do that. Today I felt as if I'm turning the corner slowly.'

Unfortunately his 85 wasn't the start of the form reversal we'd all been hoping for. Tubby had averaged just 17 in the Test series against West Indies and his poor run would continue in South Africa. Throughout his ordeal he showed great leadership qualities with his attitude and his demeanour never changing and with public support for him never wavering, judging by the letters and faxes he received.

Tubby had runs being hit all around him, with Matt Hayden compiling 112, Matthew Elliott 74 and Stephen 69. With all these runs being scored at Cape Town, I was glad to finally get a start against the modest Boland side at Paarl on a ground located amid the Drakenstein Range in the heart of vineyards an hour's drive north of Cape Town. There was a good crowd of 8000 with more black faces than white, which is good for the game in South Africa. Barbecue smoke was everywhere as the locals cooked their lunch of boerewors, which means farmer's sausage. I opened with Tubby and it was great to be hitting the ball so well in my first game since the Perth Test. It was only a small ground so I really went for it, hitting six sixes and four fours in 101 at better than a run a ball.

In one over from leg spinner Wayne Truter, I hit three sixes off his first three balls. If that didn't make him feel bad enough, someone from the crowd yelled out to him 'You're a circus' and from then on the Bolanders seemed to juggle just about every catch that came their way. Sixes were the order of the day, with Warney going for two against the big-hitting Test veteran Adrian Kuiper, a local apple grower.

It was Warney's first game back and he'd managed to forget his run-up. A couple of weeks' rest can do that to you no matter how many Tests you've played. In the end, we made 3–319 and got them all out for 269. It was a pleasing return to the crease for me. I don't have many sessions in the nets, I don't have to hit the ball a lot to be in fair sort of form and I'd much rather go out there in the middle and do my thing than concentrate on net practice. Although the standard of the opposition wasn't great, the hit-out was just what I needed for our next match, a far more important four-day first-class game against Natal in the exotic coastal centre of Durban, a city that looks something like Surfers Paradise.

The Kingsmead ground had been a favourite of mine since I hit an unbeaten ton there in the Test match on the previous tour. It's a small ground with inviting boundaries and against Natal I hit 124, coming in when our blokes were 2–70. Dale Benkenstein, the Natal captain, pushed five fieldsmen onto the fence at one time when I was giving it to his spinners. I hit a few sixes from off-spinner Pat Symcox, a veteran with a hot temper. Pat once threw an Indian autograph hunter into a swimming pool. But while he looked a bit upset as I was serving it up to him, most of the time he just stood there applauding as the ball went over the fence. He and I would meet again on tour and I must say I enjoyed facing him.

I didn't regard this game as great practice for the First Test because the bowling simply wasn't terrific. Derek Crookes bats at four for Natal and was the leading wicket-taker in first-class cricket in South Africa for the season until then. But his offies didn't seem to turn much and I got 16 off one over, including an on-drive that cleared the fence. Paul Reiffel broke down with his crook hamstring, but Bevvo bowled so well that Benkenstein, who hit 103 in the first innings, rated him as 'more difficult than Shane Warne'. Benkenstein went after Warney a bit, but couldn't play Bevvo's deliveries nearly as well. In fact, all the Natal guys seemed to struggle when Bevvo was bowling. What a difference a few months can make. In India, Bevvo could hardly land the ball on the pitch and now he was turning out to be an unexpected trump card. Our eight-wicket win over Natal gave us four out of four on tour.

During the match, I made the comment that I thought South Africa had shot themselves in the foot by trying to hide Klusener, Pollock and Paul Adams from us in the lead-up games. The trio were banned by South African officials from playing against us before the Tests and ultimately I think the move backfired badly as all three were robbed of some vital practice. Obviously the South Africans wanted to keep their trump cards close to their chest and not give us a look at what they had to offer before the Tests. It certainly didn't affect us, as fast bowlers are fast bowlers and we had seen enough of Adams and his strange style of spin bowling to know what to expect from him.

Before the First Test, Benkenstein told the papers: 'If I had anything to do with it, the Test wicket would be very grassy. They should prepare it that way to suit South Africa's pace attack which is our strength and the one edge we have over Australia.' Maybe someone should have listened.

The First Test—The Wanderers

'Dad did instil a hardness in me and always pushed me to go to new levels. He'd always say the runs which came after a hundred were going to be the easiest.'

GREG BLEWETT AFTER HITTING 214 AT JOHANNESBURG

It was nine o'clock on the biggest night of Greg Blewett's life and he was flaked out. The Aussie team had gathered at the home of our mate Rory, one of our bodyguards on the 1993–94 tour, and now part of the security team around Nelson Mandela. Rory had thrown open his house to us for a dinner on the third day. Greg had scored 156 not out but it was all a bit much for the man of the hour. Blewey's girlfriend Jodie had rung him at Rory's house at eight o'clock to congratulate him. An hour later, Greg was out to it. Who could blame him for not being the life of the party on this, his biggest night?

Greg had just played the innings of a lifetime, batting all through Day 3 of the match with Stephen and going on to post a partnership of 385, the fourth highest ever by an Australian pair. It was only the 10th time that a wicket had not fallen in a day's play in a Test match. It was an exhilarating innings for him and an exhausting process. Before that, I don't think I'd ever played a full day of cricket and not seen a wicket fall. I can only hope to find out one day just what a marathon innings of that kind feels like.

Greg has been so pumped up by adrenalin and emotion after finishing the third day's play that he'd gotten just 90 minutes sleep coming out for Day 4 to eventually post 214. Over and over in his head he played every ball he faced on that Wanderers wicket, and in the 90 minutes of sleep, I guess he literally played another dream innings. Normally Greg's a pretty laid-back bloke, but during this knock he was so hyped up that while he feasted on the South African bowlers out in the middle, all he could digest off the field was bananas. My advice to him is to stay on that banana diet because it worked a treat. It helped us to a mammoth victory by an innings and 196 runs.

Greg's a bit like me. He doesn't get too hassled; doesn't get bogged down with too many theories on batting. I played golf with him a few days before the Second Test and he's a terrific player with a handicap of four and a nice easy relaxed swing. On the cricket field he doesn't seem to worry too much and if the ball's there to hit, he hits it. But in this Test match he, like most of the blokes from either team, was on the razor's edge. It's always a plan for any team in a Test series to try and dominate from the very first session of a campaign and we did that through the spirited bowling of Glenn McGrath in the first session of Day 1 at the Wanderers. It was the batting of Greg and Stephen, however, that so thoroughly demoralised the South Africans before their home crowd. Like any good Test match it was a match of ups and downs until our two marathon men took the South African bowlers by the scruff of the neck and beat the life out of them.

THE FIRST TEST—THE WANDERERS

At the end of Day 1, South Africa had fought back from 3–25 and then 8–195 to make a respectable 302. They showed a real hardness and a readiness to scrap that at times was lacking from the West Indians in Australia. We knew this series was going to be a fight to the finish. By the end of Day 2 the match was evenly poised with us at 4–191 in reply. But by the end of Day 3, with Australia at 4–479 and Stephen and Greg having compiled unbeaten tons, South Africa were no chance.

For Greg, his commanding innings was a great morale boost for a keen, young bloke who's had his ups and downs over the years. He had been in good form all summer and we expected him to do well against the South African bowlers because he has always had a good technique against the pacemen. He sees the ball early and has a good hook and pull shot. But after just 90 minutes of sleep and a million replays in his mind following his huge effort on Day 3, he wasn't seeing anything too clearly. He may have been on 156 not out, but it's safe to say he wasn't particularly proud of his batting on the fourth morning of the Test. Allan Donald repeatedly beat him outside the off stump and then slammed a short one into his helmet. 'It was the best thing that happened to me,' Greg said later. 'I woke up feeling dreary and flat and I batted a lot better after I got hit. I'm proud of myself that I could keep going for so long.'

Greg went to South Africa with a reputation for not playing spin well, but I think that's unfair media criticism more than anything. He's been out to Mushtaq a couple of times and Afridi knocked him over with a faster ball in Adelaide in the one-dayers. But those blokes are terrific bowlers and got plenty of other batsmen out as well. I've actually played Sheffield Shield matches against Greg when I've seen him play the spinners really well and deep down I think he knew that any perceived inability he had against spin was really a myth.

In any case, Tubs took him aside after stumps on the second day, when Greg was just three not out, and told him that he was playing Paul Adams as well as anyone in the side. That really lifted Greg and by the end of the next day he and Steve were still there, having put on 288 runs in a stand that left the local lads looking pretty ragged. Greg's innings at the Wanderers was a great one, but not the best I've seen from him. He had a bit of luck go his way and he looked a little shaky early on. I think he'd only made six runs off something like 58 balls. He certainly played some great shots, but at times it looked like he might have gotten out.

Stephen was a real mentor to him out in the middle. He told him to grind them down and be patient and Greg just stuck to his task, played aggressively against Adams, using his feet to hit him over the top and took on the fast bowlers. To make a double century in a Test match is really something special and I would dearly love to emulate him one day. Stephen and Greg were simply magnificent in a partnership that left both men physically drained. Stephen's lucky red handkerchief got plenty of work wiping away the sweat that went into his 160. It was also interesting that the two batsmen who shared in the last stand which went through a full day in a Test match were at the ground. Tubby Taylor and Geoff Marsh scored 329 against England at Trent Bridge in 1989.

The First Test laid the platform for what was a magnificent series by the whole team, our first series victory in the republic for 40 years. We dominated with bat and ball in the first two Tests, and if anything summed up our early assault against South Africa it

THE FIRST TEST—THE WANDERERS

came in their second innings at Wanderers when Daryll Cullinan came out to bat. He had been making a big thing in the papers, answering speculation that he was Warney's bunny by saying that Shane didn't worry him a bit.

When Daryll came out to bat, Warney was literally licking his lips. He came over to me and said matter of factly: 'I'm going to have this bloke for breakfast.' A couple of balls later, Cullinan was out for nought. In a way, that incident summed up our early stranglehold on the series. Our last visit to the Wanderers in 1993–94 had been an unhappy time. South Africa had won the match and Shane Warne and Merv Hughes had both been fined $4000 for a couple of blow-ups. Back on that tour we had Border, Boon, McDermott, Tim May and Dean Jones and on our 1996–97 tour we were obviously putting to the test a vastly different team.

They call the Wanderers the Bullring because of the blood-curdling atmosphere there. The crowd is pressed in right on top of you. It can be quite intimidating because they're certainly not the friendliest bunch of spectators and they sledge better than Bankstown boy Paul Keating used to in Parliament. They lump us in with the Kiwis and trot out all the old lines about being sheep shaggers.

The crowd on the first day was disappointing for the organisers with just 8000 people in a stadium that seats 28,000. The ground had already hosted one Test there for the season against India and the South Africans have shown they're much more willing to support the one-day game than the five-day. We weren't upset about the small crowd because we fielded on the first day when the hecklers were scarce. By the time the crowd built up over the weekend, our blokes were out in the middle posting record scores and well out of earshot from the locals.

The first day's play really showcased South Africa's frail shell and steel backbone. Our plan to hit them hard early was carried out brilliantly by Glenn McGrath, who had them tottering at 3–25 after grabbing 3–10 from his first 10 sizzling overs. Glenn bowled as well as he had all summer, which is saying something. The wickets tumbled quickly. I took a pretty straight forward catch in the slips to get rid of Jacques Kallis and then one at short cover to get rid of Hansie Cronje. That ball was a bit difficult to pick up because the seats at the ground are very dark and when the ball comes flat it's hard to see. I took it right in front of my face and Dean Jones gave me a huge wrap on TV. But Jonesy gets carried away sometimes, and it wasn't a hard catch at all. Cronje batted stubbornly for his 76, taking 33 minutes to get off the mark, and he inspired the South African lower order with his grit, but his technique didn't look great.

Before the match, we had spent two hours studying videos of the South Africans in our final team meeting and had resolved to unsettle Cronje with short-pitched bowling. We had received some good mail from the Indian quicks, Srinath and Prasad, that Cronje didn't handle the short stuff all that well in the previous series against the Indians. Prasad took 25 wickets against the South Africans in the six-Test twin series and Pigeon was keen to carry on their campaign of terror. But the skipper proved to be a role model for South Africa's bulldog spirit.

At 8–195, South Africa were on their knees, but we knew before the series started that their strength was the fact they batted all the way down the list. Dave Richardson came in at No. 9 and he

THE FIRST TEST—THE WANDERERS

showed the same adversarial qualities he displays in the courtrooms of Port Elizabeth, where he is a high-flying legal eagle. Compared to the West Indies, whose last four couldn't bat, the South Africans have plenty of sting in their tail.

Shaun Pollock lived up to the big advance billing he had received and was very aggressive, hitting eight fours in his whirlwind 35. Allan Donald was more threatening with the bat in that match than he was with the ball, punching the air whenever he made a good shot. Paul Adams came out swinging and giving plenty of cheek as if he was the best batsman in the world. Adams hit the headlines a couple of years ago as the first coloured player to make it into the South African side. His unique action, which has been variously likened to a frog in a blender and a man trying to change a hub-cap on a moving car, has ensured he has received maximum exposure for his minimal talents.

There was plenty of youthful enthusiasm in him out on the field. He was shooting his mouth off at Pigeon and Warney and not really worrying about who he offended. McGrath bounced him first ball, hitting Adams on the helmet, but not even that could shake the enthusiasm of this little bloke. He even tried the reverse sweep on Warney, a shot he had been practising for some time in the nets. It was a frustrating time for us as Richardson and Adams repeated their efforts from Newlands on England's 1995–96 tour when their last wicket stubbornness turned the final Test and gave South Africa the series.

Buoyed by their fighting spirit, South Africa were no doubt feeling on top of the world after Day 1. Richardson was quoted as saying Australia were just another side, overrated back home. 'The Australian media builds them up to be the best,' he told reporters, 'eventually you are seeing Shane Warne's googly spinning a metre. When you get down to play them, you realise they are good, but just another team.'

Now they were fighting words.

I think it was a wise thing for Richardson to say, geeing up himself and his team-mates not to be overawed. But I reckon he might have changed his opinion over the next three days. The South African pacemen, Donald, Pollock and Klusener, weren't all that threatening on what was a fairly placid pitch. If anything, the fast bowlers bowled a bit too wide in the first innings. The main culprits were Donald and Pollock, who didn't really make full use of the new ball and didn't make us play anywhere near as much as they should have.

The Wanderers wicket became very good to bat on once the ball had lost its shine. I think the South Africans tried to prepare a fast wicket but the wicket square in Jo'burg wasn't solid underneath so they couldn't get a fast, hard and bouncy wicket. They were very worried about the pitches they were playing on throughout the series and Ali Bacher and Bob Woolmer were forever on the phone to all the groundsmen trying to ensure fast wickets to suit the speedsters.

'We had been asked to leave a bit more grass on this time,' the Wanderers groundsman Andy Atkinson said, 'hopefully to give a bit more help to the bowlers.' Obviously the South Africans were not confident of winning on any other sort of surface. In the wash-up, the Wanderers wicket was a little on the slow side and the faster the ball came onto the bat the more you could use the pace of the ball for the cut shots and pulls. South Africa really needed to get a couple of early breakthroughs, but Donald certainly didn't

THE FIRST TEST—THE WANDERERS

bowl anywhere near his best in that first innings with the new ball.

Tubby Taylor looked the best he'd looked all summer when he went out there to face the first few overs. He hit a four off his pads and one through point and his balance looked great. He was eventually out for 16, chopping the ball onto his stumps—a little unlucky.

I was quite impressed with the pace of Klusener, and the way he kept barrelling in, even though things weren't going his way on an unco-operative track. Klusener at times bowled faster than Donald and earlier in the season was clocked at 154 kilometres per hour—that's just 6 kilometres less than Jeff Thomson's world record. His nickname is Zulu and it sums up the fighting nature of a guy from rural South Africa who learned to speak in the Zulu tongue before he learned English. Klusener's approach to the game is rudimentary—he tries to bowl every ball as fast as he can and hit every ball as hard as he can.

Shaun Pollock didn't bowl anywhere near Klusener's pace, but he had more success at the Wanderers. Pollock's an eager-beaver type and a dead ringer for Richie Cunningham out of 'Happy Days'. He has a long, high action and whips his arm and wrist in his delivery stride, but he wasn't anywhere near as threatening as the other blokes. Still, that didn't stop him from giving me two sharp bouncers as his welcome to the Bullring. The next day, Ali Bacher said they were the two fastest balls Pollock had bowled all season. The first one I picked up early and just swayed out of its path, but with the second ball—that I didn't really see at all—I was just glad to have survived. I hadn't faced Shaun before and it takes a little while to get used to the action. We'd just lost the wicket of Matt Hayden for 40 and obviously the South Africans were cranking it up a bit in the hope of getting another quick wicket.

The South Africans didn't fight hard enough when they had the ball. They certainly didn't field as well in the match as their reputation dictated and my first boundary in the series came off an Allan Donald misfield—a sure sign that the whole team was down a little and not really concentrating on the tough job before them.

My dismissal for 26 was a big disappointment. With a pair of centuries in the lead-up games as preparation, I was seeing the ball well and I knew that there were a lot of runs on that track. Donald's ball came through slow, kept down and seamed away a little and I ended up reaching for it, only connecting right on the toe. As I walked off, I realised I'd just blown the chance to perhaps post a big hundred. I guess the main thing is that someone else went on to get the runs.

Jo'burg was once the setting for the world's biggest gold rush, when an Aussie named George Harrison discovered the precious metal there in 1886. The Wanderers wicket was another goldmine for the Aussies. Matthew Elliott's dashing 85 laid the platform for our eventual tally of 8–628 and he was immediately hailed as the perfect replacement for Boonie. He scored very quickly, even hooking Donald for six, and the pace with which he scored the runs really got the South Africans on the back foot. When someone is making it look easy at the crease the whole dressing-room lifts.

To their credit, South Africa kept trying. Even though Stephen and Greg put on a great partnership, South Africa never gave up. They kept coming all the time and bowled reasonably well for most of that third day with only sore backs and sweat-soaked shirts to show for it. There certainly weren't too many easy runs out there and the boys had to work for everything they scored. 'They kept at it and saved a lot of runs,' Stephen told the press. 'We scored 288 in the day but South Africa must have cut off another 50.'

We were inspired by the Test match at Headingley in 1993 when we were 4–613 and Allan Border announced that we would bat on to thoroughly demoralise the opposition. Stephen told the media: 'I kept thinking what AB would have done. It kept me going. I passed that on to Greg. When you have got a side down, you have to keep them down and make sure they disintegrate mentally and physically.'

Even though we were miles in front, there was no reason for us to declare at the Wanderers before we did. If it looked like we were torturing the home team, we were. We knew the weather forecast was good for the last day and we didn't particularly want to bat again. Time was on our side. We thought a day and a half was plenty of time to bowl them out. You tend to get mentally exhausted after a long session in the field and we thought we'd keep them out there as long as possible.

You couldn't help but feel a little bit sorry for Andy Hudson and Gary Kirsten coming out to open the batting in the second innings after they'd spent the best part of three days in the field. Legs like jelly. Mentally not quite switched on. And out there facing Gillespie and McGrath going flat out. The speed gun at the ground recorded Gillespie at 144 kilometres per hour, one click faster than both Donald and McGrath. But I wonder how fast Dizzy might have been firing if he weren't still recovering from injury.

We expected South Africa to offer plenty of resistance but they fell rather meekly. Jacques Kallis batted quite well for his 39. He looked a good fieldsman and a handy medium-pacer and seemed a pretty good find for South Africa, even if his geography is hopeless. He is notorious for once asking what altitude he was at when jogging by the seaside in Sri Lanka and for looking out the window of an aeroplane searching for the line that marks the equator.

At the end of Day 4 South Africa were 4–99, needing another 227 to make us bat again. Cullinan, celebrating his 30th birthday, was hardly in a party mood when Warney got him for a duck. They were all out for 130 as Bevvo and Warne tore out their hearts. Bevvo finished the game with four wickets in 12 balls, spinning them all over the place and zipping them through at 90 kilometres per hour. The photographs from the match showed him following through with both feet off the ground like Alan Hurst, the Aussie paceman of the 1970s. That's how quick he was pushing them through.

Even Paul Adams, who'd suffered through 52 miserable overs for an embarrassing 1–163, was down-beat as he came out to face the music. He made nought. There was none of his first-innings bravado. In the game of cricket you can't afford to be too cocky because it can turn in your face pretty quickly. South Africa conceded that they hadn't played well on a wicket that ultimately didn't suit their fast bowling. But they were also gracious in defeat, admitting they had been outplayed by a better side. I suppose it was all a bit of a shock to them. They haven't played the best Test nations in the last few years and I don't think they really realised the standard necessary to compete at the top.

After the match, Bob Woolmer lamented his team's one-day mentality when some old-fashioned stubbornness was needed. 'We

THE FIRST TEST—THE WANDERERS

haven't played well in this Test,' he admitted. 'Australia have batted better than us and they have bowled to their field. In short, they have given us a cricket lesson. What we have to do is realise that we have to improve our skill levels by some degree to match the Australians.'

It was the worst hiding South Africa had suffered since coming back to the international game. Hansie Cronje said his boys had to improve 'by 200 per cent' to match Australia. 'I don't think we were on the same ground as them in this game,' Hansie said.

South Africa are great competitors, but in this match, talent-wise, they showed they were not nearly as good as us. Their general batting, shot making and fielding was down. By and large the bowling was undisciplined. They didn't have the touch of brilliance among their players that the Australian team could deliver, but by the same token they showed themselves to be great scrappers. They're a bit like the Windies in that they rely on their pace and if the wicket doesn't suit then they don't have a lot of variety to fall back on.

The South African fast bowlers are definitely as quick, if not quicker, than the Windies. Klusener and Donald are two of the fastest bowlers in the world, but overall they don't have the same quality about their bowling as Ambrose and Walsh. Donald's the only one with a lot of Test experience and wickets. Pollock and Klusener are only new to the game. But the South Africans have plenty of aggression and I couldn't help think that given the right conditions they could be very dangerous.

It was probably fitting that a lot of the Aussie team warmed up for this Test with a visit to a police gun club the day before. Our bodyguard mate Rory organised the jaunt for 10 members of the team, who armed themselves with some of the one million or so firearms in South Africa. Matthew Elliott was one of the stars and so was Paul Reiffel, who'd want to be a pretty good shot with a surname like that. I didn't make it to the shooting range. Guns don't really interest me.

I had other targets in mind.

The Second Test—St Georges Park

'He's got a couple of nails left and he's just hammering them into South Africa's coffin.'

COMMENTATOR DEAN JONES, AFTER MARK WAUGH HAD RACED PAST 100 WITH AN AUSTRALIAN VICTORY IN SIGHT

If we thought facing Allan Donald on a green top wicket was frightening stuff, that's nothing compared with the experience of Lulama Masikazana. He turned out against us for the Eastern Province Invitation XI at Zwide, a black township outside Port Elizabeth, where we were due to play the Second Test a few days later. Lulama missed a match against England "A" in 1993–94 because he had a prior engagement. He was being ritually circumcised by spear in the nearby woods.

Yeooouchhh. That's what I call an off-cutter.

Judging by the way he played against us, he seems to have recovered pretty well. Thankfully, some South African customs remain purely South African.

Stephen captained Australia for the first time in the EP XI match and we won by 15 runs at the Dan Qeqe Stadium, a ground named in honour of a local cricket stalwart who was once jailed for his efforts to make South African sport multi-racial. There was a great photograph taken of me with my bat raised in the air looking like I was fighting off a mob of 100 or so youngsters who had me surrounded. But it was all in good fun. I'd been fielding down on the fence when I took one of the kids' bats and started hitting them a couple of catches. Before I knew it they all charged me. Everyone had a good laugh.

One of the most memorable moments of the tour was seeing those happy kids racing after the team bus at the end of the game. It's nice to get out there and see the local kids in the outlying areas enjoy our great game of cricket. They knew a fair bit about the game too, which was surprising because I don't think many of them would have TV or newspapers. They were certainly very keen on the game.

The match at Zwide was one of two lead-up matches before the Second Test. In the other—in East London against Border—we whipped them by an innings and 105 runs, with Greg Blewett following up his Wanderers heroics with another century. I chimed in with 62 and Dizzy nabbed his best first-class figures of 7–34 on the first day. Warney missed a hat-trick by one ball and veteran South African Peter Kirsten played his last game of first-class cricket. The lead-up victories had us primed for our second meeting with South Africa and it's history now that we scored off one of the great Test match triumphs of all time, pulling off a minor miracle.

At one stage in that historic match, the situation for Australia was grim—very grim—as South Africa completely outplayed us for two days at St George's Park. By the end of Day 2, on an unpredictable wicket, South Africa were already into their second innings. With a big lead in the first innings and at 0–83 in their second, they were effectively 184 runs without loss. At that stage, South Africa looked as good a bet of winning this Test match as Octagonal would in a picnic race meeting. In the depths of despair we held a team meeting to analyse just where the hell we were going wrong.

In the first innings we had batted poorly. Tubs had deliberated about playing because of a back injury but decided to go ahead. He and Hayden were both back in the pavilion with the score at 2–13 and from 70 overs we made a piddling 108. Bob Woolmer described it as one of the 'most disciplined bowling performances by a Test attack in a long time. It was 70 overs of giving nothing away. It was fantastic.'

It was also 70 overs of us playing totally out of character. And now with South Africa holding the whip hand, defeat was staring us right in the face. I stood up at our team meeting and said a few things. 'Don't throw in the towel,' I said. 'We batted for 70 overs for 108 runs, there's no way we can play like that again. If we're going to bat for 70 overs we've got to make plenty of runs. We've got to go out there and play our shots. We've got to be positive. It doesn't matter who's bowling, Adams or Donald, we've got to attack. That's the way to take the pressure off us.'

I was fired up. 'The wicket's not that bad,' I continued. 'And, anyway, I'd rather get out playing a shot than pushing forward and edging one to the keeper. I don't think we should ever bat like that again. Seventy overs for 108 runs is not the way Australians play cricket.'

I don't know if my little speech revved up the other blokes or not, but it certainly didn't hurt my performance in that game. The

116 I scored at Port Elizabeth was the 11th Test century of my career and I'd rate it as the best Test or first-class hundred I've scored. It came at a crucial time in a vital match and ended up laying the platform for us to win the Second Test and take the series 2–0. It also added another little stick man to the lucky thigh pad I've been wearing in 10 years of first-class cricket. The thigh pad has just about been shot to pieces by the big guns of Ambrose, Akram, Donald, Malcolm and Co. and every time I get hit there the pain shoots straight through to the bone. The century in Port Elizabeth made it 61 stick men—11 Test centuries and 50 in first-class games—and just those little drawings all over it is a big confidence boost. Every time I put the thigh pad on, I'm reminded that I have the ability to make the runs.

Considering everything that was involved—the pressure of the occasion and the importance of the game and the fact we were chasing 270, batting last on a wicket that was playing plenty of tricks—all made my 116 an immensely satisfying innings for me. Chasing 270 batting fourth is not an easy thing to do at the best of times and it was a tremendous team effort on that wicket with Allan Donald in full cry and with Brian McMillan, Hansie Cronje, Jacques Kallis and Paul Adams providing the back-up. Australia's victory was one of the most satisfying moments of my Test career. At several stages of the match we looked gone for all money, but we fought back with real spirit in what was truly a team effort.

I always felt I was going to get a big score at Port Elizabeth. I'd been hitting the ball well all season and had made a couple of sizeable totals in the lead-up games. I really felt I was due to score another ton and as things transpired it was the most timely one of my career. The extraordinary thing is that I genuinely thought I was out when I was in my 60s. We were still about 100 runs short of victory when I'm sure I got the faintest feather of a nick on one when facing Adams. I was amazed that no-one even made much of an appeal—Cullinan stuck his hand up for half a shout, but that was it. It was a major shock when no-one made a noise about it—that sort of thing rarely happens in cricket these days—and I was mighty glad for a break going my way.

After the match, a lot of the cricket writers said I'd finally silenced my critics who claim I sometimes bat too casually. I'd like to think I silenced them after my century in Jamaica in 1995 and at other times, as well. I have to say it really irks me that I am portrayed sometimes as not valuing my wicket as highly as some of the other players. Just because I play my shots doesn't mean I regard my wicket cheaply. People criticised David Gower in the same way. I just believe it's better to play your natural game at all times rather than be tied down by the bowlers. I can assure you, I put as high a price on my scalp as any other batsman. Every time I go to the crease I'm doing my absolute best.

My 116 was also a boon for Greg Chappell, who showed a lot of confidence in me four years ago in England when he backed me at 20–1 with Ladbrokes that I'd score 20 Test centuries during my career. I'd like to think Greg's a fair judge, too. When he placed his bet, I'd only scored four hundreds and after Port Elizabeth I'd hit 11. If I play to my potential in the next four or five years, I can't see why I can't get 20 Test centuries. It's only two a year and that's a fairly realistic expectation in international cricket. Maybe I should have backed myself as well.

Allan Donald bowled brilliantly in the Second Test. With a bit of luck going his way he could have finished with 10 wickets. The fact that he only picked up one was truly amazing. He was very unlucky. Thank goodness. The closest Donald came to a wicket in the second innings was when I got one off the toe end of the bat to Cullinan at first slip, who dropped it. I was on 105 at that stage and as it turned out, the TV replays showed it was a no-ball. Donald fell to his knees as though I'd hit him over the head with the bat. Poor bloke.

A couple of balls later I cut him for four. Just to rub it in.

If there was one disappointing aspect of this extraordinary day it was the fact I got out with 12 runs still needed. An innings of four and three quarter hours can be mentally draining and I was feeling a bit weary by the time Kallis got through with one of his quickish inswingers. If I'd still been there at the end, I could have grabbed a stump and made sure of victory.

Losing my wicket was even more annoying than the band and schoolkids at the ground who made an almighty noise for four days singing 'Stand By Me' and 'Bohemian Rhapsody' like it was a cracked record. For half an hour it might have been all right. But in the end I was trying to concentrate in a vital match and it all became a monotonous noise, the band going on and on and 90 bus loads of kids yelling out. While some people think it created a magical atmosphere, I reckon it was actually destroying the atmosphere of a great occasion. And what an occasion. Mark Taylor was right when he told the media following our triumph: 'After this, anyone who says Test cricket is dead is a fool.'

It was a great Test match, a real roller-coaster ride of depressions and highs with the momentum changing constantly from the morning of the first day. South Africa batted first and the combination of McGrath and Gillespie ripped through their top order to have them teetering at 7–95. Dizzy was on fire. On a spongy wicket and with the wind coming off the Indian Ocean like a tornado, he had South Africa ducking for cover.

We were naturally full of confidence, but pigeon-toed Brian McMillan gave them some extra legs. Coming back from a heel injury, he brought some starch back with him and together with another fighting performance from Dave Richardson, South Africa made a good recovery to make 209. We finished the day with 10 runs on the board for the loss of Matty Hayden, caught at first slip off Pollock. The second day would prove tougher.

A year before, Geoff Boycott claimed the St George's Park strip should have been dug up, but Andy McLean the groundsman there, left some grass on it. Tubby described the strip as under-prepared and it became a struggle to make runs on it. The loss of our two openers cheaply set up a domino effect. On the second day their bowlers had us tied down and we prodded around in embarrassing fashion rather than play our natural game.

By the end of the day and even without Pollock, who'd gone off early in the piece with a hamstring injury, South Africa had dismissed us for 108 and they were 0–83 without loss. The media on both sides of the Indian Ocean gave us a work-out, saying we were flat-track bullies, brilliant on good wickets, but poor on difficult pitches and when under pressure. They said we were vulnerable in low scoring games and mocked Stephen's statement in the lead-up to the Test that 'I don't think we can be beaten in the Test matches'. Some of the critics were even writing us off altogether, leaving no doubt that we'd lose in Port Elizabeth and cop it at Centurion. But we weren't about to give the series away. We were looking crook with Kirsten and Adam Bacher unbeaten at the end of the second day. But this Test, as much as any, showed just how quickly the game can change. In just two hours and 25 minutes of the third day, South Africa went from a position of great strength to being extremely vulnerable. We took their 10 wickets for 85 runs.

Kirsten was South Africa's first casualty with the score at 87 but the turning point was Greg Blewett's brilliant run-out of Kallis. Blewett has developed an amazingly accurate arm and anyone who takes him on is a big chance of having his wicket shattered. Bacher had clipped the ball to mid wicket and Blewey had rifled the ball back, crashing middle stump in a great piece of work. When Kallis went, it was suddenly 2–98. In no time it was 3–99 and 4–100, with Bacher and Cullinan joining them back in the pavilion.

That third morning we knew we had to keep things tight and we bowled very well. Blewey's run-out set the tone for us to really lift our spirits and get on top of our game. Some inspired bowling from Gillespie and Bevvo had South Africa suddenly choking. Shane Warne renewed his rivalry with Paul Adams and when Adams tried the reverse sweep again, he only managed to lob it into Tubby's hands in the slips. Warney nearly busted his sides with some exaggerated laughing and came close to falling face first on the pitch with his guffaws. Bob Woolmer said in the papers Warney's actions were 'a little disappointing. There was no need to mock him.'

But Adams can be an annoying character.

The South Africans had to take us on without Pollock in their second innings because of his hamstring injury. But I don't think his loss was such a huge blow because he hadn't bowled all that well in the First Test and in his place Kallis bowled pretty much as

THE SECOND TEST—ST GEORGES PARK

well as Pollock. South Africa still had an impressive attack with Donald, McMillan, Cronje and Kallis, but they didn't deliver when necessary.

McMillan, who is said to look more like Gerard Depardieu than the French actor does, batted well in the first innings, but his bowling wasn't that threatening in this match. I like McMillan. He's a good competitor, but he's not the world champion sledger as some claim. He might say the odd thing but most of the time it's all in jest. Not that he had much to joke about on Days 3 and 4 at St George's Park.

We needed 270 to win but our second innings started poorly. Tubby was out with the score at 13 and Matty Hayden, struggling with Test cricket, was terribly unfortunate when he was run out in a laughable mix-up with Elliott. The TV replays showed them racing each other to the one end as though they were finalists at the Stawell Gift. I came out next with the score at 2–30 and the South Africans on song. The next ball Elliott was dropped at fine leg when Adams moved the wrong way. If that wicket had gone it would have been a disaster.

It was the lucky escape we needed and after that let-off, South Africa dropped their heads a little. I gave Adams plenty of stick during my innings, hitting his first ball for four and thumping him for a pretty big six. To me, Adams is a little overrated and has a lot to learn about Test cricket. He's a pretty cocky kid, too, so I wanted to teach him a lesson.

The state of the wicket could be seen in the fact that Dave Richardson—normally very reliable behind the stumps—had an ordinary game, missing a lot of deliveries that came his way. It wasn't an easy wicket to keep on because the ball swung a lot after it went past the bat. Ian Healy kept well, but said it was difficult to glove the ball there. Australia finished Day 3 at 3–145 with me on 54 and Stephen on 11.

On the fourth day we were five wickets down and still needed 44 runs to win with me and Bevvo at the crease when Donald took the new ball. He huffed and he puffed, but he just couldn't blow us away and with McMillan needing injections on his crook heel, the South African attack suddenly seemed hamstrung. In the end, I was out to Kallis with the score at 6–258 and Australia in the box seat. But once again the pendulum swung.

Two more wickets fell in 10 deliveries. Cullinan took a low slip catch off Cronje to get rid of Bevvo and Warne was l.b.w. to Kallis. The nightmare of Sydney in 1994, when Fanie de Villiers led South Africa to a five-run victory, loomed large in our minds. We were 8–265, five runs short, and our hearts were in our mouths.

All of a sudden, the game was hanging in the balance. We'd gone from cruising to spluttering. Jason Gillespie played out Kallis's over and Heals then padded back Cronje's first two medium-pacers. Then he played the shot he'll remember for the rest of his life. Cronje's third delivery came into the pads and Heals got onto it effortlessly, hoisting it high over the square-leg fence.

Six and all over for South Africa.

We had handed Cronje's boys their first home series defeat since their re-admittance to the Test arena. Ian has only hit about two sixes in his career and it was a minor miracle when he nailed that one. To win a Test match like that was just an incredible buzz, maybe the best I've had in Test cricket. Going for that shot was a huge gamble because we were eight down and if he'd been caught on the fence the only man we had still to come in was Glenn McGrath. Would you gamble a Test series on his batting?

As soon as Heals hit it, I knew it was a six straight away. It was an immense feeling of relief. Out in the middle, Heals raised his arms in triumph and he and Dizzy embraced. In the pavilion, we were just about doing handstands and there were hugs all round. As a kid, Ian's mum Rae had given him some advice: 'Never hook or pull, son, until you're well set.' This time Heals decided to break the rules.

'It was a lottery,' he admitted to the press, 'I just watched the ball and played the moment, which is what we are all taught.' Heals admitted he was aiming for a different spot to hit the winning runs. 'The big thing was that Hansie Cronje took second slip out and put him at mid wicket. If he pitched outside off-stump I was going to try and run him through gully. But the ball drifted onto my pads and I thought I would go with it.' And perhaps, most remarkably, he admitted he didn't try to hit it for six, but looked at the ball after he'd whacked it and said: 'Geez, that's gone.'

Even though Heals had been the one hitting the winning runs, there was no prouder man in the Australian camp than Tubby Taylor. Despite all the bad press he'd received, all the calls for his head and his dreadful run of outs, Tubby never lost sight of the big picture, never lost his composure or his solid demeanour.

'It's undoubtedly the biggest Test win I have played in by an absolute mile,' he said, not long after releasing Greg Blewett from a bear hug. 'There is no better Australian side I have played in than this one.

'I just can't think of a win which rates with it.'

After the victory, I was presented with the Man-of-the-Match award and a couple of days later, Stephen and I were rated the two top batsmen in the world. One writer, describing my easy-going style, said I greeted the news with 'the nonchalance of a man who had just won a chook raffle at the local pub'. Really though, I was over the moon. It's a great honour and I guess it's unheard of for two people from the one family to be the top two in the world. We were ahead of a bunch of damn good batsmen as well.

Before the tour started I mentioned that I would like to eventually have a Test average around the 50 mark, and that still stands. There is plenty of work to be done until then, but I have received some tremendous support from fans in Australia and from the fans in South Africa, too. While I was being presented with the Man-of-the-Match award, a couple of little kids were on the TV, holding up a cardboard sign that they'd painted. It said, 'Mark Waugh is the best'. No matter how much I try to deny it, the other blokes still believe I paid those kids to do it.

The Third Test—Centurion Park

'Now remember, you blokes, no temper tantrums.'

SUSPENDED AUSTRALIAN VICE-CAPTAIN IAN HEALY TO A BUS FULL OF
JOURNALISTS OFF TO A MEDIA CRICKET DAY

The celebrations after our victory at Port Elizabeth had hardly died down when we faced the biggest threat of the tour. A mammoth hurdle in the shape of the biggest bloody elephant you've ever seen.

As you'd expect, the celebrations following our series win left a few of our blokes with 10-Aspro headaches. We were all feeling pretty crook, but decided with the Third Test starting in a couple of days, we'd get out and see some of the countryside rather than lie around in bed all day. We decided to go big-game hunting with our cameras at a national park called Shamwari, about an hour's drive from Port Elizabeth.

So off we headed—me, Stephen, Tubby, Andy Bichel, Greg Blewett, Matty Elliott, Col Egar, the tour manager, and our scorer Mike Walsh. There's nothing quite like being in the African bush. Roaring along through the scrub in two Jeeps, we saw plenty of wildlife—lions, giraffes, rhinos, buffalos, elephants—especially elephants. One bull male we encountered seemed to be pretty aggressive, so our driver, who might have thought he was Tarzan in a previous life, decided to go in for a closer look.

Good move!

Some of the blokes in the Jeep started whistling and yelling at the elephant. They'd have been safer taunting Curtly Ambrose. Suddenly the elephant turned and charged us. It was pretty bloody frightening. The elephant's ears were flapping all over the place and his trunk was jumping up and down. I yelled to the driver: 'Move. Just bloody move.' And—at the last minute—the driver took off. The elephant's trunk got to within about two feet from where Stephen and Andy Bichel were sitting. If the driver had stalled the Jeep it would have been a bigger disaster for us than the Third Test. At Centurion Park—the newly created ground on the outskirts of Pretoria—South Africa simply displayed too much hunger for us. Like that bull elephant, they were full of aggression. Only this time we didn't get away.

In some ways it was difficult to get motivated for the third and final Test, after we'd wrapped up the series. The euphoria had been immense. It was the first time an Australian side had scored more than 200 runs to win a Test since we made 6–260 against the Kiwis in 1985. At St George's Park, no side had made more than 215 to win. It had been one of the great comebacks in Test history. At one stage, even the bookies offering 8–1 for Australia to win couldn't get a nibble.

The subsequent game at Centurion was an immense comedown. Ian Healy had thrown his bat around at Port Elizabeth, hitting a six and becoming a national hero. He threw the bat again at Centurion and copped a two-match suspension.

THE THIRD TEST—CENTURION PARK

Heals, found guilty of dissent, became the first Australian to be suspended by the ICC. But really you can't blame the bloke for showing some emotion and for letting his bat reach the dressing-room before him. In a dreadful piece of umpiring by Cyril Mitchley, Heals had been given out, caught behind off Brett Schultz. The ball clearly came off his pad. And it wasn't the first time in the game. Stephen had suffered a similar fate in the first innings.

The umpiring had been terrible all tour, with them getting most things wrong. It seemed with all the drama over South Africans getting out on no-balls at Port Elizabeth, the umpires at Centurion were concentrating on the bowler's foot rather than watching the ball at the business end of the wicket. Really, it shouldn't matter that much if a bowler's foot is a fraction over the line. I think the umpires in South Africa would have done everyone a lot better service by keeping their eye on the ball. They certainly weren't biased, because the mistakes went both ways, but they made a lot of terrible decisions.

Having said that, I admit umpiring at Test level must be an awfully tough job. It's largely the fault of television. With cameras everywhere, any slip-up they make is dissected, analysed and replayed endlessly. Five or 10 years ago, a bowler could bowl a no-ball and no-one would know. Now, it's non-stop replays and the umpire spends too much time watching the crease in case there's a wicket on a no-ball and he misses it.

The incredible scrutiny umpires face over fairly minor things resulted in some major mistakes in the Third Test. The umpiring was the worst I've ever seen in a Test match. Heals' dismissal was the bitter icing on the cake. I don't think his bat-throwing was such a great crime and if you ask me, I reckon umpires should be fined for their blues. I think cricket officials are pushing the players just too far if they expect us not to react when there are so many bad decisions in one game. Enough's enough.

Heals was fuming when he came into the dressing-room and it took him a long time to calm down. It was our first loss on tour. Heals had put up with dodgy umpiring all season and in the end he'd finally had enough.

It appeared that South Africa had also had a gutful of defeat. They are a proud lot, and in the Third Test they showed tremendous grit and determination. Obviously we went out there wanting to win and to take the series 3–0, but I suppose it was mentally difficult to get motivated for that Test after the great win just a couple of days earlier. South Africa played pretty well, but we were in the game until Hansie Cronje whacked a rapid 79 in their first innings.

Cronje came in at No. 7 and was batting with the tail. It was a bit like a one-day game for him, in that he could play his shots. If they come off great; if not, it didn't really matter. He had nothing to lose. The field was spread and the pressure was off with not many guys around the bat. It really suited the way he plays his cricket. Cronje is not a great Test batsman, but in those situations he hits the ball pretty well. He, and the ever-aggressive Lance Klusener, hit 68 in just 59 minutes and Cronje and Allan Donald whacked 37 in 32 minutes. Showing the same fightback they had shown on the first day at Wanderers and the first day at St George's Park, South Africa recovered from 7–262 to make a match-winning 384. Cronje's innings included a big six over cover point when he charged Glenn McGrath, and a searing four through the covers off Jason Gillespie. You have to remember that our bowlers were pretty tired. We only played two fast bowlers in the Third Test and they were backing up from the previous Test only a couple of days before, so we didn't have a great deal of firepower.

I was bowled by Donald for only five in the first innings and in the second Symcox got me for 42, which was a devastating blow. I think my wicket was fairly crucial because at that stage Stephen and I were batting along fairly well and we had some chance of getting a lead if I'd been there at stumps. But it wasn't to be. I'd made a big hundred against Natal earlier in the tour, largely with the help of Symcox's bowling, and on the Centurion wicket I thought it would be easier to get after him than Donald and Schultz. I love a punt, but this time my gamble didn't pay off and eventually we were all out for 185. They needed just a few runs to wrap up the match. I have to give the credit to South Africa.

Symcox and Schultz, the new guys in the side for the Third Test, gave them a great deal of renewed energy for the match. Both players are prepared to back themselves. And both play with plenty of confidence. In the first two Tests, I think South Africa's young guys were intimidated by us to some degree, but when Symcox and Schultz came into the team, I think they more or less said, 'Come on, we're as good as these blokes, let's go out there and prove it.'

The change of attitude made a noticeable difference to the way South Africa attacked the Third Test—attack being the key word—even though it took Adam Bacher 50 minutes to break his duck in the first innings. Ninety-four overnight, he then spent 85 minutes in search of his maiden Test century, only making two more runs for his trouble. Bacher had predicted when he went to stumps on 94 that it might take him a full session to crack the ton. He wasn't exaggerating. When he finally fell four runs short of his goal, it had taken him 449 minutes to make 96 runs. 'I've just tried to bat for as long as I can,' he said, in the understatement of the match.

Much has been made of claims that our morale was low because Hayden, Elliott and Langer were being sent home after the Test to make way for some new blokes for the one-dayers. The fact those guys were going home shouldn't have been upsetting because we knew at the start of the tour some players would not be staying for the full journey. The team was asked whether they wanted to be told before the Test or after the Test who was going to miss out and the players said 'tell us now'. They all wanted to know in advance. Really, I don't think it should have had that big an effect, although Matt Elliott later claimed it harmed his concentration and you could tell in the rooms that he wasn't taking it well. During the match he looked a little down and he was unusually quiet. Normally Matt's a pretty jovial guy, but not in this game.

At Centurion, the juicy wicket would suit the bowlers. Generally, it was a hard tour for the batsmen, with difficult wickets in the last two Tests. Elliott received some brutal treatment from Allan Donald, who really opened up with some ferocious deliveries. Donald finally got some luck in the last Test of the series, picking up eight wickets, including 5–36 when he skittled us in our second innings to earn Man-of-the-Match honours. Donald also took his 150th Test wicket in that match, his 33rd Test for South Africa. He didn't bowl any better than he did in the Second Test, but this time he was well rewarded.

Schultz, whose career was thought to be over because of a series

Heals leads us onto the field in Cape Town for the first time as Captain in one day internationals in South Africa.

A tense finish as Tubby watches us edge towards victory against South Africa in the 2nd Test at Port Elizabeth.

The cut shot is one I love to play. Here in Port Elizabeth during the 2nd Test.

Warnie and I often take each other on with the golf sticks and managed to get a few rounds in while on the South African Tour *(left)*.

The three 'Ws'. Warne, Waugh and Waugh. Probably out in front on a team run in East London, South Africa *(below)*.

An enthusiastic Aussie team stretches out in training during the South African Tour.

A little souvenir shopping in Johannesburg.

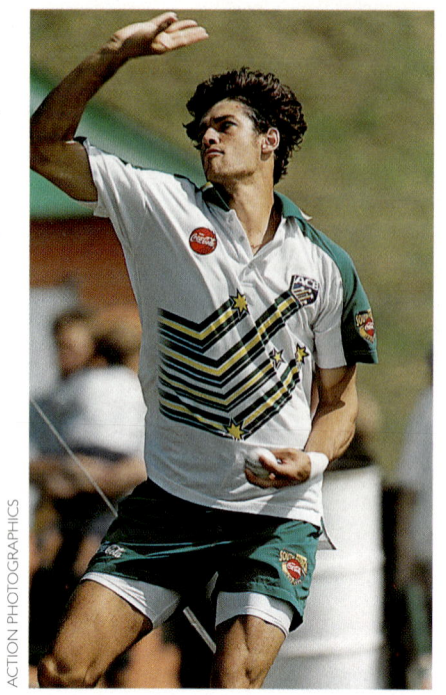

Brendan Julian, Matt Hayden and myself at training.

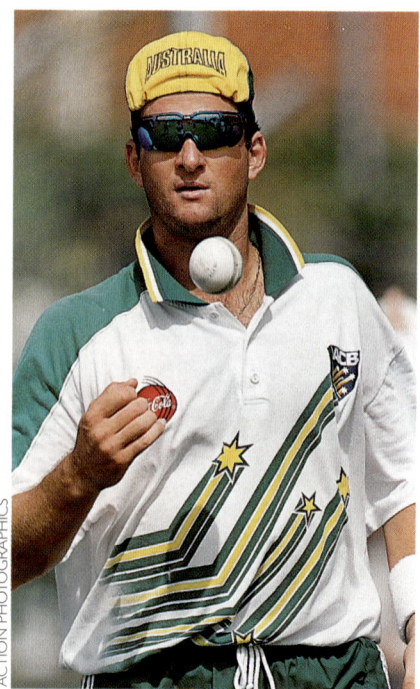

THE THIRD TEST—CENTURION PARK

of injuries, proved to be a real inspiration for South Africa. The fast leftie, who only made the side in the absence of Shaun Pollock, picked up four wickets in our first innings of 227 and bowled with plenty of fire.

Early in the proceedings English umpire Merv Kitchen got caught up in controversy. Stephen was out to Schultz on 67 as Kitchen raised the finger after a catch by Richardson down the leg side. The ball came off the pad. Kitchen also raised the finger to l.b.w. appeals off Schultz to dismiss Bevan and Warne in the space of four balls. Heals let the umpire know what he thought, but Schultz told reporters the secret of his success. 'There were times when I thought my Test career might be at an end,' he said. 'But my motto is "never give up". If I break down, I will come back again.' The same motto might have applied to South Africa.

Tubby scored his best Test innings of the tour, 38, but it wasn't easy going. There were some milestones for Australia that helped relieve the pain of defeat. When Gary Kirsten edged a McGrath outswinger into Heals' hands, our keeper had snared his 300th Test catch. Only Rod Marsh (355) has more and who knows how long that figure will stay the record? 'I think the 355 will be in my reach,' Heals told Robert Craddock. 'If I play long enough, I will pass Rod but I would like to do it in a similar number of Tests. It is more a goal for me to play 100 Tests than the 355. No keeper has ever played 100 Tests. Rod would have done it without World Series Cricket.'

Heals has pulled off some amazing wickets behind the stumps over the years, but he rates a diving one from a Ravi Ratnayake leg glance in a Test against Sri Lanka in 1989–90 as his best catch and a stumping to dismiss England's Graham Thorpe off a wide Shane Warne leg spinner as another favourite dismissal.

The Centurion Test also saw Brian McMillan, who usually heaves them around lower in the order, elevated to No. 3 in South Africa's line-up. He made 55 before I managed to score a rare wicket with my offies. The days when I could bend my back as a paceman and let them go at 130 kilometres per hour are long gone, but I still like to chime in with the ball when I can.

Glenn McGrath took 6–86 in South Africa's first innings, the sixth time in 28 Tests he had taken five or more wickets in an innings. But on the other hand Warney went wicketless for the first time in 44 Tests.

Nothing could dislodge Cronje, though, and when the loss of Taylor and Matt Hayden to another Schultz l.b.w. came cheaply in our second innings, the platform was laid for South Africa's win. The architect of their triumph in Sydney in 1994, Fanie de Villiers, watched from a light tower perched high above us. Fanie was up there raising money for charity and maybe the memories of Sydney boosted South Africa's performance.

Bob Woolmer said: 'It's a little bit after the horse has bolted, but I think we're beginning to learn how to play a five-day Test match.' Cronje, gracious in victory, told the media after the match: 'Our players have learnt more in the last two weeks than in their entire cricketing careers'. There! We knew we'd teach South Africa a lesson.

The One-dayers

'I just love watching Mark Waugh bat. I enjoy it even when he scores runs against us ... he is great.'

FORMER INDIAN CAPTAIN MOHAMMAD AZHARUDDIN

Our tour of South Africa was a great triumph for me personally and more importantly for the Australian cricket team. Even though Tests were suspended between the countries for a long time, our 2–1 Test series win goes into the record books as the first there by an Australian team since Ian Craig's side in 1957–58. It went a long way to squaring up the ledger after the 1970 tourists lost 4–0 against a side that also contained the names Bacher and Pollock, although from an earlier generation.

The 1996–97 Test series showed once again that South Africa will fight to the finish. But really, a three-Test series win could never be quite as satisfying as an Ashes tour, simply because of the limited number of matches. After our big win in the First Test, it became very difficult for South Africa to gain the upper hand. A five-Test series would be a much better indication of how the two teams compare. The only problem is the South African summer coincides with summer in Australia and if we played a five-Test tour there it would mean we would miss a whole summer of cricket at home. They face the same problem coming here. Perhaps, in the future, the administrators could look at having a five-Test series split between the two countries.

Our win in the Test series was a tremendous achievement for everyone involved and victory in the Castle Cup one-day series was the icing on the cake. It was a relief to get back to winning one-dayers after a lean trot because we have a very talented side, but one which had been letting itself down since the World Cup. Last summer, playing Pakistan and the Windies, we definitely threw games away when we were in winning positions, thinking that victory was just a foregone conclusion. After a while we figured it didn't work like that.

The thing you have to remember in one-day cricket is that the 50 overs brings the teams closer together in terms of performance. It's not like a five-day game when there are a lot of overs and the game ebbs and flows. One-day cricket is like a 100m race; there's not much difference between the bloke who comes first and the bloke who comes last. But in the marathon, the field is much more spread out. It's the same as a Test match; it's the true test of a team's endurance and ability.

Last year, our fielding dropped off a little and we missed catches and run-outs that could have won us quite a few one-day games. We also suffered a little from overconfidence and the sheer unpredictable nature of the game; an unpredictable nature that always gives the underdog a chance. Even the bottom teams, such as Zimbabwe, are capable of giving the top sides a shake, which they did in the tri-series with India and South Africa before our tour.

THE ONE-DAYERS

Going into the one-day series against us, I don't think South Africa picked their best team. I think they should have opened with the experienced pair of Hudson and Kirsten and I think they should have played Fanie de Villiers, that tough old campaigner and inspirational character who, in an eventful life, has survived having his face blown up and recently having his hand mangled by a lawn mower.

South Africa had an awesome record over the last couple of years in one-day cricket and were very confident before meeting us. Before the series began, Bob Woolmer was quoted as saying: 'One-day cricket sides have been stereotyped. I felt that anyone with a little bit of nous or thought could change that and start taking the opposition to the cleaners a bit. As for all-rounders, if you go in with five or six bowlers and nine batsmen, you've got more of a chance, haven't you?' It didn't quite work out as well as Bob had planned, despite him having a talented team. While South Africa were very disciplined in the field, their batting was like Kojak—a little thin on top.

Our one-day campaign began at Buffalo Park, East London on March 29 and the match showed why South Africa are the best fielding side I've ever played against. I know they looked ordinary in the field in the First Test, but it's difficult to stay enthusiastic when you're having 600 runs hit against you. At Buffalo Park, the South Africans were simply stunning.

I missed the match with a back injury. From time to time, I suffer a sharp pain down my right leg from an inflamed disc which is pushing on a nerve. But watching the Aussie wickets tumble was even more painful. Stuart Law, Stephen and Bevvo all scored 50s, but the South African fielding was out of this world. Stephen fell to a great run-out by Herschelle Gibbs and at one stage we lost 5–15. Among the dismissals were Hansie Cronje's run-out off Greg Blewett and Adam Gilchrist being caught short of his crease by a great throw from Jonty Rhodes.

'Those three run-outs turned what looked to be a 260–270 game—when we were nicely placed at 120 for two—into a 220 match, and that was the difference,' Tubby told the media after the game. 'You're always going to take your chances in a game like this, but Herschelle Gibbs and Jonty Rhodes are perhaps not the guys to take those chances with.'

Cronje, in his assessment of the match, said: 'The three run-outs were the turning point, but Daryll and Jacques batted superbly.' They sure did. Cullinan had the ball on a string for an unbeaten 85 and Kallis made 63 in a six-wicket victory.

Two days later at Port Elizabeth, where I'd made my Test century a few weeks earlier, the ground was good to me again and I hit 115 to help Australia to a seven-wicket win that squared the series. It was a good toss to win because the wicket was a little bit damp in the morning and Adam Dale bowled very well, at one stage taking 3–5. Conditions were a bit like he's used to at the Gabba—the wicket was a little green, the weather was humid and the ball seamed around quite a bit. Kallis was back in the runs with an 82 and Rhodes 57, but South Africa's 8–221 was always gettable.

Tubby came out swinging when it was our turn to bat, but he couldn't middle them. He was lucky not to be given out caught behind off Cronje, but at least he could see the lighter side of it. He came up to me in the middle of the pitch with that big, easy grin of his and said: 'If I'm going to go, I'm going to go down swinging.'

'Why not?' I replied. And we had a laugh in the middle of the wicket. He eventually fell for 17. I brought up my century at Port Elizabeth with two sixes off Symcox, revenge for getting me out at Centurion in the Test match. It was the first time I've brought up a century with two sixes in international cricket, but I did hit a six to bring up a first-class double century for Essex a few years ago. By going from 91 to 103 in two deliveries, I effectively eliminated the nervous 90s, but really, I wasn't even thinking about that. At that stage I was hitting the ball well and since it was only a small boundary and I was hitting with the wind, I knew I only had to whack the ball half decent and it was going to go over the fence. We made the runs with five overs to spare. It's important to be an entertainer in cricket because without entertainment value the kids will stop coming and the game will die off. You've got to please the fans.

While that century was a very satisfying innings for me, I crashed in a bloody heap in the third one-dayer at Newlands in Cape Town on April 2. And I mean bloody.

Tubby left himself out of the side saying: 'Everyone knows I haven't been batting that well so I saw myself as almost a free wicket.' Everyone hoped a break from the pressures of the game would restore his form and confidence. But at Newlands we had our own problems to worry about. When the team needed a big score from me, I didn't even bat, having had six stitches inserted in a torn hand that kept me out of the side for two matches. I dropped a catch at first slip off Jason Gillespie with the ball coming like a bullet. It wasn't a hard catch, but when I looked down at my hand there was blood everywhere. It was the first injury I've had in 10 years of cricket besides stress fractures in my back, so I guess I was due for one. The ball hit me in the middle of the hand where I'd had a bruise for a couple of weeks after taking another fast one. I guess the flesh there was tender and weakened. I looked down at the spilled ball and there was a big gash in my hand, split through the fingers as well. I went straight to hospital and came back to see South Africa making us bleed some more.

Jonty Rhodes hit an unbeaten 83 in that match as South Africa made 245. Every time Jonty did something the crowds would cheer. Every time Warney did something they'd jeer. Warney really copped it from the crowds in South Africa, and Newlands was no exception. Because of his very success, Shane draws a lot of attention and people in South Africa still haven't forgotten the run-in he had with Andrew Hudson on our tour there in 1993–94. Or, for that matter, the way Shane laughed at Paul Adams' reverse sweep at Port Elizabeth.

Every chance they got to hassle him, the crowds gave it to Shane. When Jonty hit a six off Warne, someone in the crowd even got up waving a Union Jack, no doubt lending some English support to the South African taunts. His detractors love to see Warney fail, but unfortunately for the opposition it doesn't happen too often. It's always hard for Shane because he has the attention on him constantly. He behaves remarkably well, and it's only the odd occasion that he has lost his cool. Jonty was clearly the crowd favourite in his scrap with Shane at Newlands and he took a points decision.

With my hand stitched and bandaged, I waited nervously in the stand, wondering if I would be called on to lend one good hand. Rudi Bryson, who had batted lustily in South Africa's innings, bowled with plenty of heart and got Stephen first ball. I was ready to come out to bat if we'd got to about 200 and Bevvo was still there, but he fell with the score at 8–170. With his dismissal the game was a lost cause. If I'd gone out to bat I'd probably have only opened up the stitches. At that stage it wasn't really worth the risk. In Tubby's place, Ian Healy was back leading the side after his two-match suspension and it was not the glorious debut for his captaincy in the series we'd been hoping for.

My hand injury forced me to miss the next two one-dayers, but at least having the week off allowed my sore back to have a bit of a rest and on the last week of the tour I was able to get out to the Sunday races in a private box. I was lucky enough to have the biggest punter in South Africa in the box as well and he tipped me five or six winners. I ended up winning about $400. That helped relieve some of the aches a little bit.

It was a pleasure just to be a spectator when Adam Gilchrist again demonstrated what a great striker of the ball he is in the fourth one-dayer at Kingsmead. Shaun Pollock got Man of the Match, but really Gilly deserved the award because without his innings we wouldn't have been in the contest. At one stage we were 4–50 and then 5–83, but thanks to him, we ended up making 211 and he gave us all a confidence lift with a mighty six off Allan Donald.

At one stage South Africa were 1–81, but then Warney got Cullinan, and Andy Bichel ripped through the middle order. Shaun Pollock, who'd taken four wickets in our innings, made a whirlwind 41 off 37 balls, but it wasn't enough and they were all out 15 runs short. 'The series has still got a lot of twists and turns left in it,' said Ian Healy. Fortunately for us the twists and turns went our way.

Michael di Venuto took Man-of-the-Match honours in our next one-dayer at the Wanderers, with a rapid 89. He'd been unlucky in the other games when he got run out and in fact he should have been run out at Wanderers when he was on four or five and Dave Richardson missed a golden opportunity. But Mike was very aggressive in a game that really suited him.

We made 258 and despite half-centuries by Cullinan and Kallis, they could only make 250. 'We're disappointed we couldn't get there,' Cronje said later. 'We thought it was a gettable total and when Shaun Pollock and I were there and we needed seven an over, I thought we would get there quite easily, but we lost a couple of wickets and the guys coming in were under too much pressure.'

South Africa were now staring at a 3–2 scorecard in the best-of-seven series, but as Ian Healy said: 'We've fought back twice now from being one down and I'm sure South Africa are capable of doing exactly the same. We're going to have to be right on our mettle at Centurion.' We were. Although, after South Africa made their highest ever score against Australia of 284, and I went out there and made nought, I thought we were no chance.

The lights at Centurion were the worst I've ever played under for a one-day international. They were terrible. Also, there was smoke coming across the ground from all the barbecues the South Africans love so much. For the first 10 minutes you couldn't see the ball, but if you survived that you were okay. The conditions were wet and cold, which made it really hard for the fieldsmen, so that once you got set, it became easier to score runs. Cullinan and Cronje looked like they'd put together a match-winning partnership in their innings, but Bevvo and Stephen batted superbly for a record fourth wicket stand of 189. Bevvo was

THE ONE-DAYERS

superb, hitting 103 off just 95 balls in an innings that won us the match and the series.

Strange as it sounds, in situations where you're chasing a score like 280 you've got a better chance of getting the runs than if you're chasing 220, the reason being that you have nothing to lose and you go out there playing your shots. You relax and you're not worried about getting out because you're not expected to win anyway. At Centurion Park on 10 April, we went out there and just had a hit, and it worked. Winning the match and the series was a tremendous victory for Australian cricket. It rendered the last match a non-event and I don't think South Africa were too keen on playing.

I knew there'd be some big scoring because it was a good batting wicket at Bloemfontein. Lance Klusener put in a Man-of-the-Match performance with a flying 92 to kick off their innings of 310, beating their previous record against us set in the match three days earlier. In the end, we fell 100 runs short, despite a fighting 91 from Stephen, captain of the side. But there wasn't a great deal of joy in the South African camp. Our tour of South Africa had ended with a loss, but it took none of the shine off a great campaign in which we won both the Test and one-day series.

The tour to South Africa was one of the most enjoyable I've been on because the players just seemed to click and the results, both personally and as a team, were fantastic. What really helped—on and off the field—was the great camaraderie between the players.

You never really get used to leaving home, even though the life of a professional cricketer is all about living out of a suitcase and jumping on a plane every few days. It's hard saying goodbye to my fiancee Sue for a couple of months at a time and it's hard for someone like Stephen, who's just had a little girl, to be away from his family. Justin Langer just got home in time for the birth of his little girl and Ian Healy has missed the birth of two of his three children. But that's the nature of this business.

Touring in a cricket team can be a tough job, but it does have a lighter side. This year Stephen, Justin Langer and Matty Elliott were in charge of our social committee which hands out fines for indiscretions on tour. We put everyone's name in a hat and drew out one each. You had to buy a shirt for that person—the worst shirt you could find—and believe me there were some pretty ordinary numbers. Mine wasn't too bad—it was a flowery denim thing—but some of the blokes, such as Stephen, ended up with see-through women's blouses that came halfway up their stomach. Dizzy Gillespie ended up with a figure-hugging brown and orange blouse that made him look like a refugee from the flower-power era.

If you were in a generous or really light-hearted mood, you could even go further and buy accessories to match the shirt. Andy Bichel had a really tight safari suit and Stephen bought Col Egar a blue, purple and green striped zip-up shirt with a cap that looked like a tea cosy. To our surprise, Col didn't think he looked all that bad.

Glenn McGrath, though, wasn't too thrilled with his outfit. Every Monday night you had to wear the shirt to the fines meeting and there, the big penalty was handed out. The bloke who'd made the biggest blue of the week, such as coming to training late, had to wear his shirt to a local pub or club. Glenn looked a little out of place having dinner at our hotel in Durban, but he looked totally ridiculous when we went for a drink at the pub with me tagging along as an observer.

There was Australia's premier fast bowler—one of the tough, fire-and-brimstone brigade, the successor to Lillee, Thommo and Big Merv—propped up at the bar in a tight, flowery women's blouse with a matching yellow and black hat. He copped a ribbing from everyone in the pub for about 20 minutes, but then beat a retreat back to our hotel like he was trying to stop a boundary off his own bowling. When you're on a cricket tour you take every laugh you can get.

It can be a lonely existence. I usually call home every two or three days, but some of the guys get so homesick they're on the phone every day, racking up huge bills. Sometimes you just sit in your hotel room wishing you were back in Australia. Perhaps that's why the officials made the tour of South Africa so hectic, not giving us too much spare time for reflection.

On the few days off we had between games, I'd try to hit the golf course. I ended up playing four or five times in South Africa, including a hit at the Sun City resort, one of the most fabulous gambling centres in the world, the Vegas of Africa. Sun City hosts a million-dollar tournament every year and has two top-class courses. Golf is a favourite pastime for cricketers and I always like to play Warney because he bets up big and I usually beat him. He plays off 14 and I'm off eight. Sun City is about two hours from Jo'burg and although we were there for two days, it rained on both, so I only got to play seven holes. But the casino was there, so at least we had a punt.

Overall the South African tour was a great success, winning both trophies and producing some fine individual performances along the way. Glenn McGrath had to go home with a foot injury and some of the top order batting was patchy, but winning the series more than made up for these. But the one-dayers weren't Glenn's prime objective with the Ashes tour coming up. If you asked him what he'd rather do, limp through a one-day series in South Africa or be our pace spearhead on an Ashes tour, it wasn't a hard choice to make. An Ashes tour is the pinnacle for any Aussie cricketer.

Australia v. South Africa

This is my report card on the performance of all the players involved in the Tests and one-day internationals during Australia's 1996–97 tour of South Africa

AUSTRALIA

MARK TAYLOR
3 TESTS   80 RUNS AT 16.00 (AV.) HIGHEST SCORE: 38
2 ONE-DAYERS 24 RUNS AT 12.00   HS: 17

Tubby had a summer he would probably like to forget. But he's captained the side tremendously. He has very good player management skills and is able to make the right decisions at the right time.

MATT HAYDEN
3 TESTS   64 RUNS AT 12.80   HS: 40

Along with Tubby, Matt found it hard work against the new ball on bowler friendly tracks. In South Africa, Matty looked a little nervous and tentative at the crease and was disappointed with his results. A player averaging 60 at first-class level has obviously got the ability to succeed at Test level.

MATTHEW ELLIOTT
3 TESTS   182 RUNS AT 36.40   HS: 85

Although he didn't score a mountain of runs, he looked like he was in good form. I think he has the ability to make 5000 Test runs for Australia. He looks the complete player with his temperament and technique. He is more than capable of representing Australia at one-day level.

MARK WAUGH
3 TESTS   209 RUNS AT 41.80   HS: 116
1 WICKET AT 38.00
4 ONE-DAYERS   118 RUNS AT 59.00   HS: 115 NOT OUT
0 WICKETS FOR 16

I was happy with my form in the Tests and the one-dayers, disappointed that I missed out on a big score at Jo'burg, but delighted with the two centuries at Port Elizabeth. Being elevated to No. 2 on the world batting ratings behind Stephen was a great thrill, though ratings and averages aren't everything to me. I hope my Test innings at Port Elizabeth proved once and for all how much I value my wicket. I think I've been misunderstood as a batsman. I might make it look easy out in the middle sometimes, but believe me, batting against quality bowlers is never easy. If I make it look that way, then it's just a visual thing. I like to change the flow of the game when I'm batting. If we're in trouble and I can score quickly and change the flow of the game, then to me, that's just as important as the number of runs you make.

GREG BLEWETT
3 TESTS   271 RUNS AT 54.20   HS: 214
1 WICKET AT 74.00
7 ONE-DAYERS   148 RUNS AT 24.67   HS: 53
3 WICKETS AT 55.67

Greg has played extremely well since his recall to the Australian team. He's a player who doesn't get weighed down with too much theory. He just goes out there and bats aggressively. His 214 at Jo'burg was a gem and one to savour.

STEPHEN WAUGH
3 TESTS   313 RUNS AT 78.25   HS: 160
1 WICKET AT 20.00
7 ONE-DAYERS   301 RUNS AT 50.17   HS: 91
0 WICKETS FOR 25

After South Africa, he was still sitting on top of the world batting ratings. He's as solid as a rock in the middle order. He batted well in the First Test and again in the Third. He's been so consistent. His form hardly waivers. He might have one bad innings now and then, but not too many of them. You can always count on Stephen to make runs.

MICHAEL BEVAN
3 TESTS   72 RUNS AT 18.00   HS: 37 NOT OUT
9 WICKETS AT 19.55   BEST: 4–32
7 ONE-DAYERS 297 RUNS AT 59.40   HS: 103
1 WICKET AT 203.00

For my money, Bevvo was the player of the series in the one-dayers and should have got the award ahead of Shaun Pollock. Despite the fact he bowled very well in the first two Tests, he would rather be regarded as a Test batsman. He was disappointed with the way he batted in the Tests. In the one-dayers, he came out and absolutely smashed them. I think he just has to go into the Tests with that same attitude. If he does, he'll make a mountain of Test runs. He's just a little unsure of himself at the moment as a batsman in the Test arena.

IAN HEALY
3 TESTS   57 RUNS AT 14.25   HS: 19
11 CATCHES
4 ONE-DAYERS 56 RUNS AT 28.00   HS: 25
2 CATCHES, 1 STUMPING

Heals was great again behind the stumps. He didn't make as many runs as he would have liked but his keeping was second to none. You tend not to notice him behind the stumps, but his keeping to the spinners on this tour was top shelf, especially to Bevan. If you put another keeper in there, they'd be scurrying and dropping balls, but Heals makes it look so easy.

SHANE WARNE
3 TESTS   11 WICKETS AT 25.63 BEST: 4–43
6 ONE-DAYERS   10 WICKETS AT 27.20 BEST: 2–36

Warney took a lot of big wickets. He's not going to get 30 wickets every series, but he bowled well throughout the series and always kept the pressure on their batsmen. And he certainly took the honours in his battle with Cullinan, helping swing the series our way.

GLENN McGRATH
3 TESTS   13 WICKETS AT 22.23 BEST: 6–86

Glenn bowled very well in the first and final Tests. He was down a little on pace in this series, I guess because he was nursing an injury and was holding back a little. But like Curtly Ambrose, he never gives an inch to the batsman. He's always at them, probing and opening up weaknesses. Day in, day out, he's a very consistent fast bowler who rarely yields a bad ball.

JASON GILLESPIE
3 TESTS   14 WICKETS AT 20.50 BEST: 5–54
6 ONE-DAYERS   8 WICKETS AT 30.88   BEST: 2–39

To me, Dizzy was the find of the tour. Before the series, I tipped he'd go very well, given the pace he displayed in the nets and in the few spells he delivered against the West Indies. He's as fast as anyone I've faced, certainly in the top bracket for sheer pace, and I think he and McGrath could form a pretty lethal combination for Australia for quite a few years to come.

PAUL REIFFEL
4 ONE-DAYERS 1 WICKET AT 170.00

I guess you'd have to say he was unlucky not to make the initial selection for the England tour. I thought he was a pretty sure thing for the Ashes, but he didn't bowl a great deal in South Africa and I suppose the selectors took into account the injuries he's had.

ANDY BICHEL
4 ONE-DAYERS 8 WICKETS AT 24.75 BEST: 3–43

He had a frustrating tour because he bowled well at times, but couldn't get a crack at them. He's a lion-hearted cricketer and a fine third seamer in any Test team.

MICHAEL DI VENUTO
5 ONE-DAYERS 150 RUNS AT 30.00 HS: 89

He looked very aggressive at times, but suffered a couple of run-outs that could have seen his average climb a lot higher. His 89 in the one-dayer at Johannesburg was a match-winning innings that put us 3–2 ahead and in sight of the series victory.

STUART LAW
7 ONE-DAYERS 145 RUNS AT 20.71 HS: 50
1 WICKET AT 52.00

Stewie would have been disappointed not to have converted several good starts into big scores in the one-dayers. But he's a player of immense natural talent who has a lot to offer Australian cricket. He should never be regarded as a one-day player only.

ADAM GILCHRIST
6 ONE-DAYERS 127 RUNS AT 31.75 HS: 77
2 CATCHES, 1 STUMPING

Gilly is one of the best strikers of the ball in Australia and he looked very exciting in the one-dayers, hitting 77 at Kingsmead in an innings that included five boundaries and two sixes.

ADAM DALE
7 ONE-DAYERS 8 WICKETS AT 34.38 BEST: 3–18

He had a good season in Australia and carried it on in South Africa. He's very accurate and quite deceptive because he has a fair bit more pace than you realise. He hits the pitch quite hard but combines it with good control. He can swing the ball either way and has a very good bumper. In most of the one-dayers, he was our best bowler, and the only time he was hit around was in the last match of the series when the South Africans were going for broke.

BRENDON JULIAN
1 ONE-DAYER 2 WICKETS AT 26.50

We didn't see much of BJ. He flew all the way to South Africa to play in one 50-over game after the series had been decided. At least he can be confident with the knowledge that he is still very much in the minds of the Aussie selectors.

JUSTIN LANGER

Justin's a very good tourist and a good team man who gets on with everyone. It was frustrating for him because he only played a handful of games on tour. A player we would all love to see succeed at the top level.

SOUTH AFRICA

ANDREW HUDSON
1 TEST   31 RUNS AT 15.50   HS: 31

Hudson was harshly treated by the South African selectors. He was dropped after the First Test and we never saw him again. It was pretty rough since, at age 32 and with more than 30 Tests behind him, he is an experienced opener who has done well against us in previous campaigns. South Africa needed some experience at the top of the order and I thought he could do the job. He was batting quite well in the second innings in Johannesburg when he was run out. He is a funny sort of player in that he looks good, but then gets out when you least expect him to. I was surprised that he got dropped from the Test team, but he can take some consolation from the fact that he was named in South Africa's squad to tour Pakistan in October.

GARY KIRSTEN
3 TESTS   82 RUNS AT 13.66   HS: 43

Kirsten and Hudson have been a very good opening combination for South Africa in recent years, both in Test cricket and in the one-dayers. Kirsten was out of form for the Test series and got dropped for the one-dayers, which was a big blow considering he had been called the best one-day player in the world and had some huge scores behind him. We expected him to be a tough player to get out, but he didn't live up to his reputation and despite his one-day record, South Africa left him out of their team for those matches. We thought the opening partnership would be one of South Africa's strongest areas, but in this series, Gary just didn't look like making a big score.

JACQUES KALLIS
3 TESTS   49 RUNS AT 9.80   HS: 39
5 WICKETS AT 26.80
7 ONE-DAYERS   237 RUNS AT 33.86   HS: 82
2 WICKETS AT 97.50

This bloke is a player with a lot of potential. He can bat in the middle order and bowl with good pace and swing. He didn't make that many runs in the Tests, apart from the 39 in Johannesburg, but his technique looks very solid and he only needs a couple of big scores at Test level to get the necessary confidence that will lift him. He has all the shots, but he was pretty nervous out there and it was difficult for a 21-year-old in that side when you consider that the Second and Third Tests were played on wickets suited to fast bowling. It wasn't easy to make runs there, but he looked exciting in the one-dayers.

DARYLL CULLINAN
3 TESTS   122 RUNS AT 24.40   HS: 47
7 ONE-DAYERS   334 RUNS AT 66.80   HS: 89

Cullinan reminds me a lot of Greg Ritchie in that he is a great stroke maker. He has the most talent of the South African players, but in the Tests he wasn't prepared to build an innings. He'd get to 20 or 30 and play a flashy shot. You'd have to say that Warney still has the wood on him a little bit. Cullinan makes runs against other Test teams and has a good international record, but he seems to have a mental block when he plays against us. Still, he was prolific in the one-day series.

HANSIE CRONJE
3 TESTS   204 RUNS AT 51.00   HS: 79 NOT OUT
4 WICKETS AT 23.50
7 ONE-DAYERS 251 RUNS AT 50.20   HS: 80
4 WICKETS AT 48.50

Cronje was the backbone for much of South Africa's success. But we watched film of him during the last series against India and he looked vulnerable. He was backing away. His technique has really fallen off against fast bowling. He made 76 in the First Test, but he looked ordinary to me, in fact he looked a little scared—playing from outside leg stump. But he is a good striker of the ball and if he gets going he can score runs quickly, which he did in the Third Test to set up a face-saving victory for South Africa. He plays Warney reasonably well—positively. His technique wasn't good, but he made runs.

He is quite a defensive captain who plays by percentages. He will defend rather than attack and tries to tie up the game and hope that the other team makes a mistake. He is not the man who will have three slips, a gully and bat-pad. He is more likely to have two slips, a gully, and spread the field around. He is a good communicator to his players, but a fairly defensive captain just the same.

JONTY RHODES
1 TEST   30 RUNS AT 15.00 HS: 22.
7 ONE-DAYERS   185 RUNS AT 37.00   HS: 83 NOT OUT

Jonty played the First Test and then the selectors got rid of him until the one-dayers.

I think Jonty is short of Test class as a batsman. He looked very 'iffy' at the crease in Johannesburg, very jumpy. But he is a very good one-day player as his record against us showed.

The 50-over game suits him down to the ground because he can nudge hard and run between the wickets and, of course, his fielding was outstanding in the one-dayers. He is enormously popular in South Africa, a very affable bloke who is always signing autographs. He is always smiling and seems to enjoy his cricket a great deal. A good friend of mine.

SHAUN POLLOCK
2 TESTS   66 RUNS AT 22.00   HS: 35
4 WICKETS AT 27.75
7 ONE-DAYERS   152 RUNS AT 38.00   HS: 41 NOT OUT
12 WICKETS AT 21.42   BEST: 4–33

He played particularly well in the one-dayers and has definitely got a lot of promise as an all-rounder. As a batsman, he has a good technique and watches the ball closely. Despite his reputation as a speedster, he only bowled medium-pace in the Tests as he was coming back from injury. In the one-dayers he was starting to hit the pitch a bit harder but he is not genuinely quick.

LANCE KLUSENER
2 TESTS   39 RUNS AT 13.00   HS: 30
4 WICKETS AT 46.25   BEST: 2–23
3 ONE-DAYERS   119 RUNS AT 59.50   HS: 92
5 WICKETS AT 23.60   BEST: 3–41

This bloke is genuinely fast—as quick as Donald and Gillespie—with real aggression and raw talent. He was playing bush cricket only three years ago and he still approaches the game the same way. When he bowls, he just charges in all day, with plenty of ticker and when he bats he is like a big hitter from the country. He lines everything up and tries to hit each ball as hard as he can. There is not much subtlety with his batting. He doesn't play the spinners well, but against the fast bowlers he is very aggressive and goes for his shots.

DAVE RICHARDSON
3 TESTS   124 RUNS AT 41.33   HS: 72 NOT OUT
12 CATCHES
7 ONE-DAYERS   13 RUNS AT 3.25   HS: 8
5 CATCHES

A real fighter, Richardson batted well in the Tests. He put in big efforts when they were down and out at Jo'burg and Port Elizabeth. Richardson is a very gifted player. Most of the time he doesn't look like he is putting a great deal of effort in behind the stumps, but he certainly has gotten the results with his batting and keeping. In this series, he didn't keep anywhere near as well as he has done in the past. Generally, he makes it look real easy behind the stumps, but he dropped more balls in this series than I've seen him do before. I suppose, at 38, age is starting to catch up with him.

ALLAN DONALD
3 TESTS   11 WICKETS AT 29.54   BEST: 5–36
7 ONE-DAYERS 9 WICKETS AT 31.56   BEST: 3–67

The Second Test was one of the worst hard-luck stories I've seen in cricket. I've never seen anyone bowl that well and walk away with only one wicket. Donald could easily have had 10. He is a real class act. Once he gets on top of you, he can be devastating. But by the same token he has been known to struggle if he doesn't get things his own way. At 31, he is still very quick, with great control and a beautiful action. He's a tremendous fast bowler to watch so long as you're not at the other end.

PAUL ADAMS
2 TESTS   4 WICKETS AT 58.50 BEST: 2–66

At this stage in his career, I think Paul is a little overrated and I don't view him as a danger at Test level just yet. He's only young so he may improve with experience, but at the moment he bowls too many loose balls, relieving any pressure. He has quite a following in South Africa, being the first non-white Test player.

ADAM BACHER
2 TESTS   161 RUNS AT 40.25 HS: 96
5 ONE-DAYERS 96 RUNS AT 19.20 HS: 45

Bacher looks a limited player. He batted well in the Third Test on a difficult wicket, even if he seemed to take forever to get off the mark on the second morning when he was trying to get his 100. I give him his due for stubbornness, but I don't see him as a real potential top Test player.

HERSCHELLE GIBBS
1 TEST   38 RUNS AT 19.00 HS: 31
6 ONE-DAYERS 122 RUNS AT 20.33 HS: 33

This bloke has talent. He strikes the ball really well. In the one-day games, he hit a couple of sixes over cover and it takes a top-class player to do that. He strikes the ball very cleanly, and I think that, if South Africa give him a regular run in their Test side in the middle order, he could make valuable runs for them. It was a hard series for him because we batted on ordinary pitches. It wasn't easy for experienced guys, let alone new blokes coming in and trying to make a career.

BRIAN McMILLAN
2 TESTS   119 RUNS AT 39.66   HS: 55
3 WICKETS AT 26.00

These days his bowling is taking second fiddle to his batting. He is not the force with the ball he was a few years ago. His batting, though, is very solid and he could do a good job for South Africa coming in at No 3. Contrary to his reputation as a bit of a slogger, McMillan is actually very patient and is willing to spend a long time at the crease to graft his runs.

PAT SYMCOX
1 TEST   3 WICKETS AT 37.00
3 ONE-DAYERS   5 WICKETS AT 35.60

I hit Symcox for a lot of runs when we played Natal, including quite a few sixes. I was devastated when he got me out in the Test at Centurion. At 37, he is a veteran campaigner and a good competitor. He is a fairly good one-day bowler, but in this series we got stuck into him. We made a point of attacking him because he has bowled well against us in the past.

BRETT SCHULTZ
1 TEST.   6 WICKETS AT 15.16   BEST: 4–52

He bowled reasonably well in the Third Test, but his figures were a little flattering because he had luck on his side with a couple of dismissals—notably Stephen and Ian Healy caught off the pad. He's a confident guy with a lot of energy and he brings real spirit to the team. Despite a reputation for being injury prone, he can still bowl the odd quick ball and being a leftie he can make things awkward.

LOUIS KOEN
2 ONE-DAYERS 22 RUNS AT 11.00

He struggled a bit in both matches he played and did nothing of note.

DEREK CROOKES
5 ONE-DAYERS 39 RUNS AT 13.00 HS: 18
1 WICKET AT 156.00

Crookes is a good one-day player despite his unflattering figures in this series. He bowls steadily, bats reasonably well and, along with Rhodes and Herschelle Gibbs, is one of the reasons South Africa are such a great fielding team.

RUDI BRYSON
4 ONE-DAYERS 6 WICKETS AT 31.83 BEST: 2–34

I'm not sure why the selectors chose him in the one-dayers ahead of some younger guys. If they wanted an older, more experienced bowler, I felt they should have gone for Fanie de Villiers. Bryson is a bustling kind of bowler with good pace and he bowled well on occasion in the one-dayers. At Cape Town, he bowled Stephen first ball to take two wickets in two balls.

The Ashes Tour

'We are flippin' good at self-doubt in this country, but our aim is to develop an England team that everyone can get behind and cheer.'

ENGLAND COACH DAVID LLOYD AFTER VICTORY IN THE FIRST TEXACO ONE-DAY INTERNATIONAL AT HEADINGLEY

Jason Gillespie might have become just about the quickest thing across 22 yards of turf, but on the morning of Saturday, 10 May 1997, his brother Rob was the slowest thing on the Hume Highway.

These days, Jason lives hundreds of kilometres from his parents, Neil and Vicki, but they still support him as much as they did when he was a 10-year-old kid from Bangor battling a crippling illness. In those days, he had no earrings, no goatee and no ponytail. Just something called Guillain-Barre Syndrome, a virus that attacks the nervous system and threatened to put him in a wheelchair for life. Jason's Dad told Cameron Bell of Sydney's *Sunday Telegraph*, that after repeated trips to the St George Hospital, Jason was finally cured. He went on to become the Illawong Cricket Club's Cricketer of the Year and then moved with his family to Adelaide at the age of 10. Jason's still there, letting fly on the Adelaide Oval, but Neil and Vicki now live in Canberra.

With the Australian team taking off from Sydney airport for the Ashes tour on 10 May, it gave the Gillespies a chance to drive up and give him a family send-off. But, unlike Jason, the rest of the Gillespies apparently like life in the slow lane. They left Canberra at 5.15 am with their middle son, Rob, at the wheel. Rob was on his L-plates at the time and couldn't go more than 80 kilometres per hour along the expressway in the rain. They drove to Campbelltown, on the city's south-western fringe, took a train to the city and a cab to the airport, somehow making a three-hour journey from Sydney to Canberra into something like 7 hours and 15 minutes. They still got to give Jason an enormous surprise send-off, making it just in time before we jetted off to Hong Kong on the first leg of our journey to the greatest cricket contest the game has to offer.

From the time we got home from South Africa until we left for England, the Aussie players had only about three weeks of free time. Each of us found different ways to unwind. I played some golf, went to the Harold Park trots and shot a couple of ads for Extra chewing gum. Michael Bevan was married in Sydney in front of about 80 guests at St Andrew's Church in Manly, and Andy Bichel had Mike Kasprowicz as his best man when he tied the knot up in Caloundra. Unfortunately, there wasn't much time for honeymooning.

The 1997 Ashes campaign in England would comprise an official tour party of 17 players and five officials. It would last 110 days with accommodation and travel costs topping $1 million. Before it was over, we had stayed in 20 hotels, travelled 7000 kilometres by coach, signed 20,000 autographs, drank 3000 litres of Coke and Powerade and enjoyed a quiet ale or two and a few celebratory sips of champagne. For every member of the touring party, the trip was a dream come true—even for those of us who had gone before. Into our bag went the six Test shirts, the sun hat, the jumper and vest, the green helmet and, of course, the baggy green cap. Off we went on the greatest tour in the world.

First port of call was the Kowloon Cricket Club ground in Hong Kong, which isn't much bigger than an Aussie backyard. It's not too difficult to hit a six there and although there's a good atmosphere with the crowd so close, it can be quite dangerous for spectators. If they're not watching, they've got half a chance of getting hit in the head. In an exhibition match against a World XI attack that included some recent acquaintances in Pollock, Klusener and McMillan, I managed to hit seven deliveries over the fence, making 116 from 66 balls. We went on to win the match that had been designed to try and improve the popularity of cricket in the Asia–Pacific area. It was more a fun day than anything serious. The ground was soaking wet and we were lucky even to get a game.

Mark Taylor's frustrating run of outs even continued in this hit-and-giggle match when he was out, caught behind, off Pakistani paceman Mohsin Kamal for four after appearing to miss the ball. Tubby had gone through two series of below-par performances and even before we arrived in England, Geoff Marsh was having to go into bat for him. 'He'll definitely play in the first couple of Test matches,' Geoff said after the Hong Kong match. 'He's the tour captain and we're just really hoping that Tubby can find some form.'

The whole team echoed that thought as we touched down in

England, a place I'm very fond of, after having spent four and a half seasons playing for Essex. I really came to love the country. The money was good and for a young cricketer on the way up, there is no beating the county scene for experience. In my first season for Essex, I was playing against the likes of Curtly Ambrose and Ian Bishop and at that early stage in my career, I would not have had the chance to regularly hone my game against quality opposition back home.

England is a great tour for an Aussie cricketer, and not just for the cricket. It's a land of fantastic scenery and history. There's Wimbledon and the British Open and Ladbrokes betting shops where you can punt on just about anything. There's golf and shopping and village greens with people sipping their gin and tonics. Our main mission, though, was not to see the sights or savour the atmosphere but to defend the Ashes.

Admittedly, our preparation to retain the game's most coveted prize was pretty ordinary. On the eve of the tour I told Jim Maxwell, of the ABC, that the English players weren't tough enough or hungry enough on the field; that they were more worried about individual efforts than playing as a team. The comments made headlines around the cricket-playing world, and unfortunately in the early part of the tour it was the Aussie team who didn't perform to our ability. After losing the Texaco One-day series 3–0, we looked a pretty sorry bunch. Although the Tests were our priority, we definitely wanted to win the one-dayers too and losing 3–0 was not the best way to start a Test campaign. We let ourselves down and let our supporters down in the process.

England played superbly in the three matches, but they had the one-day home advantage of picking a specialist side for the limited-overs games. Because the majority of our big matches were to be Tests, we jetted off to England without some of the guys who would have been specials for the one-dayers at home—guys such as Paul Reiffel and Stuart Law.

We also had a fairly limited preparation for the international matches with only a few first-class games in the early part of our series in England. Our first game in England came a couple of days after we touched down in London, playing at the picturesque Arundel Castle against the Duke of Norfolk's XI in the traditional start of hostilities for Ashes tourists. The Duke's XI had a couple of old faithfuls in John Emburey and Neil Foster, but we won by 133 runs and the old Duke was pretty impressed with the way we played. He has a soft spot for the Aussies and reckoned they were 'damned unbelievable in the war ... wonderful in the desert ... toughest people in the world'.

Mike Kasprowicz took the first two wickets of the Ashes tour and Jason Gillespie dismissed Andy Flower and Andy Whittall with his first and third deliveries on English soil. For Dizzy, it was all a breeze and just the start of a cyclonic performance in the Old Dart. The match was played amid a real English-village atmosphere, with people on deckchairs around the boundary.

It was quite cold and unpleasant for playing cricket, though Tubby wasn't complaining. He hit 45, and against Northamptonshire two days later, in a damp city of red bricks and fog, he hit 76. The freezing weather made it tough, but Mark hit the ball reasonably well in a rain-affected game.

There are few countries where the cricket is so affected by the weather as it is in England. Early in an Ashes tour, it's generally wet and cold and the wickets are damp and seaming around. However, a bit later in the summer it's easier to bat because it's warmer and the wickets are drier. But it's still tough adapting to wickets that are a lot slower with more seam than we're used to playing on.

My hand, which was sliced open in the one-dayer at Cape Town, was still aching in the cold weather and I took a spell from fielding in the slips. I gave the hand a further rest when I sat out the next match, a one-dayer against Worcestershire, in what was our third limited-overs game in four days.

We hadn't been in England for a week yet and already things were going badly. While you couldn't say the wheels had fallen off our campaign, the early part of our tour could be summed up by our team bus being stuck in the mud at the back of the Worcester ground. The bus was a state-of-the-art, 32-seat coach on loan from the Manchester United soccer club. It became a sort of mobile home for us for nearly four months as we travelled throughout the countryside of the United Kingdom.

It was decked out in the distinctive red and blue Manchester colours and bore the number plate M3 UFC. Warney took the seat normally reserved for United's ace, Ryan Giggs, and the video player was always running with AFL or league tapes or *Ace Ventura Pet Detective*, which was played so often that the tape was just about in tatters by the end of the tour.

Worcester's ground at New Road had been under water the night before we arrived and our driver, Hughie Jones, got a bit lost and ended up bogged out the back. We lost by five wickets against a team that contained Big Tom Moody, Graeme Hick and Phil Newport and the sight of a tow truck rescuing us did little to get our team back on track.

The best thing about the early games before the Test series

started was that we met up with our old mates from down-under. We had a drink with Big Tom and Dean Jones, who was leading Derbyshire and had given his players gel-filled hand warmers to combat the cold. At Durham, we caught up with David Boon, who was enjoying his first season as captain, coach and entertainment coordinator with the perennial battlers of county cricket. Boonie really seemed to be relishing his time at Durham. For him, it was a bit like starting all over again at Tasmania in that he'd taken over an ordinary side and was trying to mould them into a top outfit.

Unfortunately, the match with Durham was rained out and we found ourselves playing the first Texaco one-day international against the Poms a couple of days later with bugger-all preparation. The lack of match practice in English conditions showed and, although we started the first one-dayer on a grim, grey day in Headingley as clear favourites, we were bundled out for 170 and they overhauled us with 10 overs to spare.

The match was a triumph for their skipper Mike Atherton, who had been under the same sort of pressure Tubby had been facing, with many in the press calling for his head. His performances since the World Cup had been ordinary and he was content to occupy the crease at one end while the other guys played their shots.

There are a lot more newspapers and a lot more critics in Britain than in Australia and a lot of them are simply looking for a negative angle. The British media can make or break players and the success of a sports person there often depends on how tough they can be in the face of criticism that is often more biting than Mike Tyson. There is no tougher arena to play the game than in Britain.

As an example, the *Sun* newspaper, which sells about four million copies a day, once had a picture of Mike Atherton's face superimposed on the body of a sheep as he led his lambs to the slaughter. If you don't perform on the sporting field in Britain, the journos and commentators rarely miss you. Going into the Texaco series Ray Illingworth wanted Atherton axed and even Geoff Boycott was calling him a 'slow coach', claiming he didn't score quickly enough. Anyone who ever slept through a Boycott innings knows this was a case of the pot calling the kettle black, or as Martin Johnson wrote, 'not unlike Ronald Biggs complaining to British Rail that his train was late'.

Atherton wasn't taking anything lying down. Before that first match at Headingley the defiant skipper said, 'I've suffered more than most at Australian hands. That's what makes this summer so special. It's our chance to turn everything around. Australia are the bookies' favourites and, on paper, the stronger side. But this game is not played on paper. We must seize the initiative early, starting with the one-day internationals, and not let go.'

The Headingley match introduced us to some of England's young lions, whose presence injected more life and fight into the side than we were expecting. England had a new selection panel for the series; one member being my old mate from Essex, Graham Gooch. Mike Gatting and David Graveney made up the panel and were known as 'The G Men'. They clearly knew what they were doing in picking several keen guys hungry for Aussie blood. The youthful enthusiasm of the new blokes gave England a leaner, keener, more energetic look in the field. The base of the team was similar to England sides of the last few years, but the young blokes gave them a much needed heart transplant.

THE ASHES TOUR

Atherton won the toss at Headingley and Darren Gough, who bowled with plenty of venom, tossed five sharp overs bowling up the slope, quickly accounting for Tubby, who was out with the score at eight. The English bowling was as tight as a carpet snake's grip and Atherton, Mark Ealham and Graham Lloyd were outstanding in the field.

Stephen and I went four overs without hitting a single run, which is not a particularly good strike rate in the limited-overs game, and I was out with the score on 39, yorked by the long and lean Dean Headley, the bloke with the best pedigree in cricket. His grandad was West Indian maestro George Headley—the little Panama-born batsman they called the Black Bradman. His father, Ron, was a left-handed opener who played two Tests for the Windies in 1973 and spent 16 years as a county player at Worcester. When asked to compare his talents with his predecessors, Dean, a lively 195-centimetre seamer, laughingly said he was already a better bowler than both of them. He certainly proved that as our innings got away from us.

We desperately tried to make runs, but Gough and that Welsh wizard Robert Croft contained us. Croft sent down 10 overs for just 16 runs, after making a gutsy decision to change his grip in the match, using a method he had only experimented with in county games. 'I changed the grip because it was so cold,' he explained in his singsong accent. 'My normal grip wouldn't have been as accurate. The new one gave me a more consistent line and length. It was an idea I picked up in New Zealand in the winter.'

Croft bowled exceptionally well in the one-dayers and, like Gough, is a real fighter, a goer who was one of the few Englishmen to emerge from their debacle in Zimbabwe with pride intact. I rated him as the best spinner in the English side before the series began and he bowls in a similar vein to Tim May, with a similar action—drifting the ball away while maintaining a good line outside off stump, which a lot of the English off-spinners don't do. In the past, they've tended to bowl too defensively and aim for off stump, but he bowls aggressively and is a good competitor, always looking to get wickets rather than contain the scoring. Like Gough, he's an exceptionally proud bloke too and his enthusiasm and energetic personality really seemed to lift the team early in their campaign. When he was first chosen for England to play against Pakistan at the Oval in 1996 he said he was doubly proud that he was representing both England and Wales on the world stage. That pride certainly had an uplifting effect on his team-mates at Headingley.

A bloke named Adam Hollioake—born in Melbourne, educated for a time in Ballarat and then based in Surrey under my former NSW team-mate Dave Gilbert—also came in to score a couple of late wickets, but it was with the bat that he really shone. I played against Adam two years earlier when I was with Essex, but he was a bits-and-pieces player then. He was a pretty good hitter and part-time bowler, but it seems that when he achieved English selection at the age of 25, his cricket really blossomed.

Adam and his tall, 19-year-old brother Ben were both in the England squad and, even though Ben didn't get a run until the series was decided, both were throwing punches from round one. Darren Gough calls the Hollioakes the 'Boys with Balls of Steel' and they are certainly a rugged pair. Adam revealed that his most treasured possession in the whole world is a signed print of his hero Muhammad Ali standing over the prostate form of Sonny

Liston. It has pride of place in the home he and Ben share in Battersea and he reckoned the conflict of boxing fired him up for the performance of his life against us in that one-dayer at Leeds.

As far as any loyalty to the country of his birth goes, well, forget it. 'We learned our cricket in England, feel loyal to this country and can't help where we were born,' Adam said, while Big Ben chimed in with, 'Neither of us will be intimidated by the Australians'. They weren't. Not in the one-dayers at least. As Atherton explained: 'When you are youngest, you tend to be your bravest, most confident, hold no fears and I'm all for that kind of attitude.'

Even though we'd made a piddling 170, we had the Poms at 4–40 before the Surrey combination of Hollioake and Graham Thorpe steered the ship home. Thorpe made an unbeaten 75 and Hollioake made an unbeaten 66 off 84 balls with five fours and two sixes. He struggled early as McGrath and Gillespie blazed away in poor light from the Kirkstall Lane end and then he edged one past Ian Healy's gloves off Warney when he'd made only five. But he showed real 'Aussie' grit, hammering a long-hop from Warney for the first of his sixes, smashing McGrath through mid-off to reach 50 off 66 balls and then sending Dizzy over the boundary fence into the Western Terrace for the winning runs. In defiance of England's new dress rules, he had even gone onto the field without a shave after having woken at 8 am and deciding breakfast was more important than appearance.

His mum and dad, John and Daria, who now live in Perth, flew in to watch their kids in action. 'I wasn't sure if my mum and dad had made it,' Adam said after toasting success. 'The first time I knew they were here was when I hit Warne for six. I looked at the replay screen and saw them on the terrace and thought, "I know those two ugly mugs".'

Foster's brewery sent Thorpe and Hollioake 131 cases of beer for their performance and the British press were drunk with excitement. Under a headline 'Adam and Heave', the *Sun* said: 'It might have lasted just one day, but victory over Australia is something to be cherished and trumpeted. What is more, it was accomplished with a highly professional performance—the sort with which Australia have been humiliating England since 1989.'

Under another story headlined 'Heart of Oake', the same paper quoted Mike Atherton saying: 'I felt during the build-up there was not much hope in the country that we could beat the Australians. Even the night before the match, people were coming up to me in the restaurant telling me England did not have a chance. This win can get everyone backing England against the Aussies.'

The *Guardian* newspaper urged its readers to 'Lie back, think of England and enjoy every Aussie-bashing, Warne-whacking minute of it'.

In less than 50 overs, Adam had been transformed into a superhero. 'I'm convinced Adam is the strongest man in the world,' wrote Alec Stewart. 'During pre-season training we had a test to see how many press-ups we could do in a minute. The average was 38 or 40. Adam did 96. He could probably lift up the entire gym and take it home with him. He is ridiculously strong. Adam and Ben remind me of the Waugh brothers. Adam is Steve Waugh, the fighter and Ben is Mark Waugh, more laid back and naturally gifted.'

No doubt the Hollioakes honed their skills competing against each other just as Stephen and I did as kids. When we were young, we were always trying to outdo each other. We were in the same teams all the way through, the same junior sides, the same rep teams. We were always trying to beat the other in backyard cricket or we'd go down the road leaping all over the place trying to top the other at tennis. We stopped trying to outdo each other when we made the Test side but that early competitive fire shaped both our games.

For the Hollioakes, it certainly produced two top-notch cricketers. With England leading the series 1–0, Adam again hit the winning runs in the next match two days later at the Oval, scoring 53 not out. We'd made a reasonable 6–249 off our 50 overs with Michael Bevan hitting an unbeaten 108 and Adam Gilchrist 53, but four of our wickets fell to run-outs and they beat us with 10 balls to spare, thanks largely to Atherton or 'Ather-ton' as the *News of the World* headlined his success. 'His Man-of-the-Match effort wasn't just to try to make Taylor's life a misery, it was a clear sign to Ray Illingworth and Geoff Boycott where to go,' wrote David Norrie.

In the same newspaper Richie Benaud wrote: 'Atherton handled his troops well again in conditions unlike those at Headingley, where the ball was swinging and seaming. At Leeds we had the vision of a new England ... the same applied yesterday [at the Oval]. There was passion in every diving save, every slide to knock the ball down and also in the bowling. Once again, Darren Gough and Robert Croft were outstanding and what a difference they are making to this England line-up.'

Vic Marks rubbed some salt into our wounds in the *Observer* when he wrote, 'Let's grab the chance to write it [the headline] while we can. I know it was only a one-day competition ... but here goes "England humiliated the Australians at the Oval yesterday".'

It didn't get any better for us two days later at Lord's. This time, Ben Holioake, who had never even been to the ground before and was frightened he might get lost on the way from the dressing-room to the middle, came out batting at No. 3 for England, swinging away in his international debut as though he were Errol Flynn, sword-fighting in some Hollywood swashbuckler. For a 19-year-old playing at Lord's for the first time, he showed no sign of nerves. He was obviously very confident in his own ability and shaped as a good prospect for the Poms. For the third time in four days, Adam Holioake hit the winning runs for England but it was Ben who stole the show with 63 off just 48 deliveries, 50 of his runs coming in boundaries.

We had made 269 all out, off 49.2 overs with Gough snaring five wickets. I hit 95, at better than a run a ball, and the outfield was so swift that I just stroked the ball and it went for four. But again England were a little too good.

The English press can savage their stars when they don't perform, but they turn on the praise like gushing fountains when there's a victory. The Holioakes became the first brothers to play for England since Dick and Peter Richardson 40 years before. In the *Express* newspaper, Colin Bateman said, 'Big Ben had the temerity to take on the Australians with a bravura performance we have not seen the like of since Ian Botham in 1981' and John Etheridge in the *Sun* wrote that Ben had made the 'most sensational entry into international cricket since W. G. Grace stopped shaving'.

'Just imagine it,' he wrote. 'Here was a 19-year-old lad, the youngest to play for England since 1949, elevated to No. 3 in front of a 28,000 full house and against the ultimate foe. That adds up to some sort of pressure. But Hollioake's response was a dazzling, breathtaking assault that will linger for ever in the memory of all who witnessed it.'

Our Ashes campaign had started disastrously. We had been out-batted, out-bowled and out-fielded by a revamped England side bursting with pride after a transfusion of new blood. We had not even made the finals of the one-day series in Australia and now we had lost three out of three to England.

The weather was yet to pick up, so it was a gloomy time for us in a gloomy place. Still, we were confident that England would not get another chance to gloat over us. We were confident they could not maintain the rage. There was no way we'd succumb in the Tests. Not a chance.

The First Test—Edgbaston

'I guess you don't [get carried away] when you've known what it's like to have a Messerschmidt up your arse.'

WARTIME PILOT AND TEST GREAT KEITH MILLER ON WHY HE DIDN'T SUCCUMB TO PRESSURE ON THE CRICKET FIELD

Could it possibly get any worse? England had belted us in the three one-day internationals and had all but drowned us at Edgbaston in the First Test in Birmingham. I was in hospital with my stomach about to explode, Jason Gillespie had broken down, Greg Blewett was hopping about on one leg, Shane Warne was rubbing a crook shoulder that seemed like it would need surgery and Mark Taylor was marching to his professional death with a million poisoned pens poised to stab him in the back.

It seemed Tubby had everything against him. After the horrors of the Texaco series, he'd lasted just four balls in the match against Gloucestershire before falling to a combination of Mike Smith and Jack Russell. Justin Langer and Matt Elliott both made centuries in that game on a tepid wicket one scribe called a 'mottled strip of Plasticine' but Warney was bowled when not offering a shot after a bird flew straight in front of him as the bowler released the ball.

In the next game, against Dean Jones' Derbyshire, our nightmare run in England continued as we suffered defeat by a wicket despite centuries from Greg Blewett and Michael Bevan. Andy Bichel broke down after just five overs. Tubby made a half-century in the second innings, but only after Jonesy dropped him in the slips when Tub was on one.

About the only good thing to come out of the match for us was the birthday cakes the county turned out for Stephen and I on the last day as the crowd sang 'Happy Birthday'. But really the birthday wasn't so happy for either of us.

It's only fair to say that we were badly underdone before the first Test match at Edgbaston, with a lack of quality three-day games. In fact, one writer said that had it been a wet weekend in Derby before the First Test, we would have gone into our first big match with England not so much undercooked as raw. The danger for us was not that we were still in one-day mode going into the Test as some critics speculated, but rather that in the lead-up games to Edgbaston we were virtually playing against attacks about equal to a first-grade Sydney club side and a week later we had Devon Malcolm, Darren Gough and Andy Caddick hurling them down at us.

Our preparation was not conducive to immediate success in the Tests and I really felt for Tubby during those first cruel weeks in England. I've known him since I was 16 years old when we were a pair of opening batsmen playing together for the Combined High Schools in Sydney. We played three junior Tests for Australia as kids and a one-day junior international and five or six times for NSW under-19s. In fact, we'd opened the batting in various teams in something like 14 games before making it into the senior ranks

The Brains Trust. Taylor and Marshy thinking about how to catch some fish in Port Elizabeth *(right)*.

Volleyball brings some variety into the never ending training routines while on tour *(below)*.

The picturesque setting of Arundel for our first game in England.

No it's not Adelaide, City of Churches, but a postcard shot of Worcester County Cricket Ground. Worcester v Australia.

Heals the best wicket keeper in world cricket. Here at Lords during the 2nd Test.

Glenn McGrath is fast becoming the Curtly Ambrose of the modern game. In action here at Arundel.

Geoff Marsh showing us the ropes at training at The Oval.

The start of worse things to come. Bowled by Dean Headley in the first One Day match in Leeds.

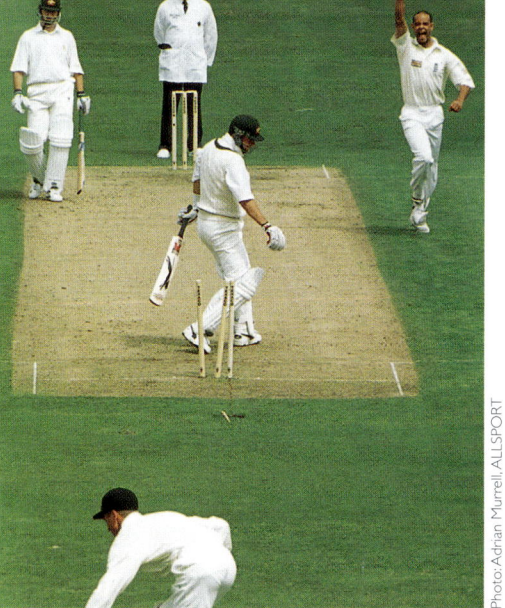

It's birthday time. Coca Cola, our sponsors, supplied us with a couple of enormous cakes.

Heals, as usual, is congratulated after a neat bit of work off Warney during the 3rd Test at Manchester.

THE FIRST TEST—EDGBASTON

and I must say it hurt to see him suffering in England, even though as kids he was always ribbing me, saying I wasn't good enough to open the batting with him.

Tubby and I even made our first-class debuts together for NSW on the windy old TCA ground high above the Derwent River and the City of Hobart in October 1985. Before that match, Bob Simpson, then the NSW coach, said we'd handle the pressure of our first-class debuts by not being overawed; just keeping our heads down and letting our natural ability shine through. In those days, Boonie's blokes had a pretty slippery opening bowler from the West Indies named Winston Davis, but as a kid of 20 years Tubby faced up to him with the same firmly set jaw and fearless attitude that would characterise him during the darkest days of his Test captaincy. Days when it seemed the weight of the world was on his shoulders.

The Tub is a man of immensely strong character and a fierce courage that belies his polite and placid public demeanour. On the surface, Tub never broke; never lost his cool or composure. Inside, he was being torn apart with all the calls for his head, all the speculation about his future and all the ugly mean-spirited newspaper stunts.

Probably the worst one came from the *Daily Mirror*, who ambushed Tub at Bristol when we were playing Gloucestershire. They rang him at the team hotel and wanted him to come downstairs to pose for a photo with a three-foot wide bat, and seemed surprised when he refused. Showing more front than Harrods, they bailed him up later in the day getting off the team coach and got a photo of him brushing past a reporter holding the wide bat. The next day under a headline 'Batman and Sobbin' they joked that the stunt was 'simply in the interests of a decent summer's sport. We want an Ashes scrap worthy of the name—not a repeat of the 3–0 one-day whitewash.' The same paper offered Tubby a one-way ticket back to Australia, but quickly withdrew the offer when they realised he could go down to the airport counter and swap their ticket for cold hard cash.

Despite his many trials, Tub never lost sight of the bigger picture. I'm sure many players would have blown their top under the circumstances, but he's ice cool and level-headed and doesn't show the strain. He never lost his dry sense of humour. Before the match with Derbyshire, and with just about every paper running big spreads highlighting Tubby's batting failures, one reporter asked our fearless leader if he was looking forward to the combination of Devon Malcolm and Phil DeFreitas. 'No,' Tubby replied. 'But I'm sure they're looking forward to me.'

He set an example for all sportsmen when he summed up the century that saved his career in Edgbaston when he told reporters, 'You have to remember it's only a game'. That's right, folks. While playing cricket for a living is a dream profession, it is still only a game and it's meant to be enjoyed. Every time I go out to bat I keep reminding myself not to get tied down by pressure and just play my natural game. Not that I wasn't feeling the pressure, stuck in the Priory Hospital in Birmingham, watching the First Test on TV as our illustrious leader went to meet his fate after our first innings when the ball had seamed around as though it were on a string.

I was confined to bed with a stomach virus that the doctors at first thought was appendicitis. I had felt crook after the second day's play and was nauseous at dinner. I woke up with fever and

THE FIRST TEST—EDGBASTON

went to the ground still feeling sick. It was really hurting me down low on the right side of my groin and Errol Alcott, our physiotherapist, took me off to the local hospital. Fortunately it was just a virus. An infection in my glands had caused swelling in the groin, which was causing all the pain.

Some unkind souls suggested that my stomach ache was due to me being force-fed humble pie over my comments about England's lack of hunger, toughness and teamwork. Really, there was no humble pie to eat because England put themselves into a winning position in that First Test by doing exactly what I said they hadn't been doing for the last eight to 10 years in matches against Australia.

In the one-dayers and then at Edgbaston, they demonstrated good team harmony and a real fighting spirit. It was obvious from the first ball at Birmingham, when Darren Gough swung through the heavy atmosphere past Tubby's outside edge, that this England team wanted to do well for each other and not just for themselves. They had decided that Edgbaston would be the start of great things.

A week or so before the First Test, playing for Yorkshire against Northants at Headingley, Gough had crash tackled a streaker as though he were Ellery Hanley defending the try line for Leeds. He was still fired up against us, and the Poms were chasing everything in the field as though their lives depended on it. They showed spring heels in jumping after some of the catches.

I've always thought England had good players, but their coach David Lloyd and skipper Mike Atherton really seemed to have injected some team bonding into the side. I don't think England were too happy under their former boss Ray Illingworth, but after getting rid of him they seemed to have lifted sharply in spirit. That spirit haunted us at Edgbaston.

Despite a late fight from Warney, our first innings ended in the sixth over after lunch on the first day. It was a collapse that the Birmingham crowd had not seen from an Australian side since 1902, back in the days when the Aussie skipper, Joe Darling, used to wrestle team-mates naked in the dressing-room and a 60-year-old playboy named Edward VII had just been crowned King of England. At one stage, we were 8–54 and by the time stumps were called, England had a lead of 82 and still had seven wickets in hand. England had started as 3–1 in the betting shops, but by lunchtime—just two hours later—they were 4–1-on favourites.

Tubby had won the toss and decided to bat and England's bowlers Gough, Malcolm and Caddick performed superbly. Malcolm was having a great season for Derbyshire and Jonesy would rev him up every time he took the new ball by telling him to get a couple of wickets for Ray Illingworth. Illingworth had a very public and bitter feud with the fast bowler after their previous trip to South Africa.

Jonesy knew all about the big fella's pace. Devon had broken his little finger in Ballarat in 1990, busted his arm in Perth in 1991 and terrorised the Aussies at the Oval in 1993. However, as sharp as Dev was, Gough was even quicker at Edgbaston. He was simply superb operating from the City End. He is the sort of gutsy scrapper England were crying out for in their attack; plenty of pace, a big heart, variation and aggression. With his jaunty walk, his short-cropped hair, his northern accent, his bustling run-up and his stocky, muscular build, he reminds me of the old footage of Harold Larwood.

THE FIRST TEST—EDGBASTON

Much to England's delight, Gough has developed pace that is sometimes blistering. He's a tremendous competitor and a real danger man who makes things happen when he bowls. On that first day, we made a measly 118 all out, but I don't think we played too many bad shots. Gough and the big Kiwi–born Caddick were really hitting the spot and, to be honest, Gough bowled as well as anyone I've ever faced. Anywhere. Ever. And Caddick certainly showed no ill-effects from the piece of surgeon's drill tip he still carries inside his left leg as a souvenir from an operation a couple of years ago that saved his career.

On that first morning in Birmingham, we were a bit out of form, but really we were simply victims of very good, tight bowling and plenty of swing. Warney saved the day to some extent, hitting eight boundaries in his 47 before skying one off Caddick to Malcolm at third man. England had 56 overs left in the day's play and by stumps were 3–200.

Mark Butcher, a sometime Test batsman and sometime rock guitarist, started well with two boundaries, but he was the second man out with the score on 16 and Mike Kasprowicz had finally picked up his first Test wicket after having been so unlucky against the Windies. He was probably our best bowler in Birmingham, but against the Windies he had been a bit nervous and didn't bowl with a great deal of speed. He really came into his own in England and over the next three months would emerge as a fine Test fast bowler. Kasprowicz's bowling was one of the few moments for Australia to savour as the game moved into the second day.

Before the series, Glenn McGrath had spoken to the press about he and Jason Gillespie developing into a combination of Lillee and Thomson proportions within three to five years. The Poms seemed

163

to delight in punishing him for reminding them of that terrible twosome.

Nasser Hussein, who I played a lot of cricket with at Essex over the years, produced the best innings I've seen from him by a long way. In fact, one of the best innings I've seen in Test cricket. The bloke who started his cricket career as an eight-year-old leggie in the Essex Schools Under-11s was batting on a fairly difficult track, but his form was outstanding. He hardly put a foot wrong, which is understandable given the fact that footwork seems to run in his family. His sister, Benazir, is a ballerina in the West Australian Ballet. Nasser ended up making 207 and by the time Warney had him caught behind, England were 6–416 and Tubby must have been contemplating a new career.

Graham Thorpe made 138 for England as well, in what was his third century in four Tests, but he always looked like he could get out while Nasser, at the other end, always seemed to be in control of the situation. Those two put on 288 and at one stage hit 135 runs in just two hours. They broke England's record for a fourth-wicket stand against Australia set way back in 1938 at Lord's by Wally Hammond and Eddie Paynter.

In the end, England declared at 9–478 and we were off to face the music again on the morning of the third day. Or rather, the other 10 guys in the team were while I was off to face what was shaping up as an appendectomy. It was a weird feeling sitting in a hospital bed watching Tubby play an innings that would change his life. If he had failed at Edgbaston, I'm pretty sure that would have been his last innings for Australia.

In the *Times* newspaper, Alan Lee had written that Tub was groping for form like a man who has mislaid his spectacles.

THE FIRST TEST—EDGBASTON

Imagine the pressure that he must have faced heading out there; his future hanging in the balance, his life's work, his career, his reputation, his place in cricket history all riding on a darting ball from a trio of fast bowlers operating under ideal conditions and with a lead of 350 runs spurring them on like a hurricane at their backs. In the 21 previous Test innings Tubby had walked out to bat, he had returned to the dressing-room without making 50. Edgbaston was do or die. His run of outs had reached the point of no return, and he just went out there saying to himself, 'I either make runs or I'm gone'.

Tubby remembered that, after all, it's only a game. Relieved of the stress that might have broken a lesser man, he got going when the going was tough. He made the runs that saved his career, compiling them in one of the gutsiest knocks you could ever hope to see. He and Matt Elliott put their heads down and England, without the alarming swing of the first day, but still with some sharp seam and bounce, were given a lesson in Australian grit. It was a momentous innings both for Mark Taylor and for Australian cricket. If he hadn't performed, a new era would have taken over, and Stephen probably would have been the captain for the Second Test at Lord's.

Malcolm bowled with good pace, but the England attack was a little wayward and Matt and Tubby were not afraid to play their shots. Even though his career was in crisis, Tubby still picked off the loose ball fearlessly and he pulled a six and four off Mark Ealham's first over. He and Matt put together a century opening partnership, Australia's first since Tubby had scored his previous half-century against Sri Lanka in 1995. When he reached 42, Tubby had hit 2000 runs against England in only his 23rd Test against them and that gives a pretty good indication of his record as a Test batsman, despite the recent slump.

When Greg Blewett came to the crease, he scorched the bowling, despite a tendon problem in his knee that had him hopping about for a major part of his innings. He charged Robert Croft, cracking him for six with a straight drive after we'd passed 200 with just one wicket down.

Tubby really had to fight for every run as he neared the century that took him from zero to hero. The Poms tightened the screws and kept him stuck on 89 for ages. When Tub was on 99 he had to deal with Mike Atherton questioning the shape of the ball and then a streaker invading the ground. Finally, though, the ton was his, and as he saluted his team-mates in the pavilion, all of Australia—in fact all of the cricket world—saluted him as a bloke with more guts than a sumo wrestler. Geoff Marsh summed it up best when he said: 'No-one could break him ... this has to equal what Kieren Perkins did [in Atlanta].' Tub's father simply remarked, 'He's a tough bugger.'

Mark Taylor's as tough as they get.

At the end of the third day, Tubby slept as soundly as he ever has and I couldn't wait to get out of hospital. I was released from the Priory at 12.45 pm on the fourth day of the Test as Tubby got ready to resume his innings on 108. Greg Blewett was on 61, but set about quickly trying to overtake his skipper, playing some cracking shots.

Christopher Martin-Jenkins gave Blewey the biggest wrap imaginable: 'Some of his fierce hooks and full-blooded drives through extra cover will have reminded older watchers of Sir Donald Bradman. The baggy green cap, the bent front knee and the bat flowing through over the shoulder seem to rise from the covers of a dozen treasured cricket books.' But all good things come to an end and Tubby's hopes of us batting all day to save the match evaporated when Croft dismissed both batsmen and then Gough got Michael Bevan.

At last, I went out to bat. I might as well have stayed in hospital. I hadn't eaten for a day and a half and had been lying down for most of the day. I had a light-headed feeling and certainly wasn't 100 per cent well. It made no difference to my batting and I probably would have gotten out even if I was feeling like I'd backed a 200–1 winner at Randwick. I copped a great delivery from Gough that lifted more than I expected. It caught my thumb and Alec Stewart did the rest.

At the start of the day's play, I thought that we had a chance to save the match, but we lost a couple of quick wickets and then, with only 120 to defend, we let them hammer the runs off just 21 overs. It was a pretty ordinary final act in a match where so much had gone wrong. As a team, we had a lot of soul-searching to do and a lot of repair work.

With Jason Gillespie injured, Paul Reiffel was recalled. Pistol had been left out of the original squad, no doubt because selectors thought he was an injury risk given the dodgy history of his knee and back. While we were all delighted with him coming over, you couldn't help but feel sorry for Adam Dale. On the day that Pistol got the call, one of the Brisbane newspapers, so confident their Queensland hero would get the nod, conducted a big interview with Adam and had taken photos of him joyously celebrating his call-up to the Ashes squad. I'm glad I wasn't the one who had to tell Adam the bad news. I'm sure it was a dead heat between the two of them. Adam and Pistol are two similar bowlers and while Adam is not as quick, he really swings the ball and bowls a great line and length as he showed in South Africa.

While we were doing a re-jig, England were dancing one. They popped the champagne corks in a victory that, coming after their 3–0 rout of us in the one-dayers, reflected the heady times in Britain. In the *Express* Marcus Berkmann credited the upswing in British fortunes on the recent election of their confident young hero at 10 Downing Street.

'I blame Tony Blair,' he wrote, '[and his] notorious Cheshire cat impersonation. Michael Atherton is a fast learner. A mere four years after being called Captain Grumpy for scowling at everybody all the time … like the Joker in Batman, Athers appears to have had his smile seared into his flesh.' A week later Mike Atherton was awarded the OBE.

Older heads told the Poms to beware, not to get carried away with so much success so soon. Mike Brearley wrote in the *Observer* that while it was a heady time for Britain, might four successive victories over Australia be an intoxicating illusion? One swallow did not make a summer. But the Poms revelled in their triumph, with headlines such as 'Wilting Matilda' and 'Didn't We Do Didgeridoo Well?' Matthew Engel wrote that, having teased England for so long and so mercilessly about new and mysterious deliveries under development, Shane Warne had revealed to England the most surprising ball of all, the one that did nothing.

The *Sun* ripped in with: 'We are talking about a cricketing earthquake, the tremors of which will reverberate across the globe for months to come. When a Kangaroo with a soft underbelly meets a rampant Lion, it's no contest.' And the *Mirror*, they of the wide-bat stunt, went full-bore with 'Don't you feel just great to be British' right across their front page.

It was a hard loss for Australia. But one we could handle. Even though we'd been beaten, we weren't heartbroken or demoralised. We knew that, just like our gritty skipper, we had the ability to fight back. We had lost the Test, but Mark Taylor had won the day.

The Second Test—Lords

'Grey skies are gonna clear up, put on a happy face.'
SONGWRITERS LEE ADAMS AND CHARLES STROUSE

I'd never be one to name-drop. But sometimes you just can't help it. The last time I was around for tea at Buckingham Palace, Queen Elizabeth and I had a lovely chat about our love for horse racing and the magic of the track. These were the days before Princess Diana's tragic death and the pall had not yet descended over the monarchy.

I asked the Queen if she enjoyed a punt and with a bit of a giggle she said 'no' in a way that probably meant 'yes, but I don't want to admit that some of the taxpayers' money gets plonked on the third at Epsom every so often'.

The Aussie team had a great time at the Palace, meeting Her Majesty and Prince Andrew, who seemed like he was a pretty big cricket fan. Not only do the Queen and I share a fondness for the horses but we also love corgis. She's got about eight and I've got one, a six-year-old called Rebel, who's always getting into strife with my other dog Kingston, who is supposed to be a Labrador but is often mistaken for a headless chook.

The great thing about being an Ashes cricketer on tour in England is that you not only get to take snapshots of places like the palace but you get invited inside too, and they make a real fuss over you. It's visits like this and that sense of history and tradition that help make England the pinnacle of cricket tours.

I love the city of London and all its tourist attractions, the great old atmospheric pubs and restaurants. Another favourite is the old Georgian town of Bath, where I once played against Somerset in a game for Essex. But for the cricket fan, you just can't go past Lord's and its Long Room, its priceless treasures of the game and the sense of history that is created at the traditional home of cricket. Lord's. What a place, what an atmosphere and what characters. The crusty MCC types still exist with their plummy accents and old boy mannerisms. One joker at Lord's interrupted Geoff Marsh during a press conference in the Pavilion and told him, 'You were the best wicket-keeper I have ever seen'. He either had Geoff mixed up with Rod or there's an aspect of Swampy's game that he managed to keep quiet all these years. At another time, someone wanted to know if our sixtyish luggage man, Tony Smith, was Ian Chappell. They look about as similar as Danny DeVito and Arnold Schwarzenegger did in *Twins*.

Unfortunately for Australia, we hit Lord's at the same time as the worst weather to hit England this century and a match I'm sure we could have won, escaped our grasp. Rain delays and wash-outs were the bugbear of the early part of the tour for us. At least, when there was no play, we could console ourselves with a game of golf. For a lot of our blokes the opportunities to hit form on the cricket

THE SECOND TEST—LORDS

pitch were scarce, but our golf games prospered. Early in the tour, we worked out that Ricky Ponting had played nine games of golf and only two of cricket. Ricky would later make the most of his opportunities in the Tests just as he did on the golf course. He shoots about even par every time he goes around and he was also in luck on the eve of the Edgbaston Test when a couple of his dogs produced the double in Launceston.

Next to the cricket, the golf courses are the biggest source of competition for the Aussie team. Most of us love the game and we take every opportunity to play. Up at Birmingham before the First Test, we played at the Belfry, where some classic Ryder Cup matches have been held. It's a favourite course for Stephen ever since the 1993 Ashes tour when he hit close to a plaque commemorating a massive drive by Seve Ballesteros. It's on the 10th-hole par 4 and you've got to hit over water to an island green about 300 metres away. Needless to say plenty of balls end up in the drink.

Unfortunately for the mad keen golfers among us, the game against Middlesex coincided with the British Open, so not only was our cricket match washed out, but we didn't get to see any of the action at Royal Troon. Probably just as well for me since I backed the Swedish fruit loop Jesper Parnevik, the bloke who eats volcanic sand and spits out new age philosophy. He got pipped at the finish by the little Texan Justin Leonard. Jesper had blown a two-stroke lead on 18 in the 1994 British Open at Turnberry and he copped it again at Royal Troon.

The odd-ball Swede's demise mirrored my punting fortunes in England. I had little Ricky Ponting sweating so much at one stage it looked like he'd swallowed a bad vindaloo after he'd given me

173

33–1 on Michael Stich at Wimbledon. Let me tell you, little Ricky doesn't like to part with a quid and he was looking a very worried boy as Stich tore through the field like he did in the 1991 final when he beat Boris Becker for the whole box and dice. I only had 20 quid on Stich, but it still worked out that if the German got up, Ricky was going to have to fork over more than 1200 bucks. Either that, or a half share in one of his dogs. But, just as Jesper Parnevik fell at the final hurdle, Stich sank against Cedric Pioline in the Wimbledon semis.

On one of the few days it was actually fine, some of us went to Wimbledon and saw Martina Hingis down Anne Kremer in the opening round. We also saw Sandon Stolle on one of the outside courts, but we couldn't get to see Pat Rafter because the crowds were packed so tightly.

The crowds are rather less congested at Lord's, where you can move around and meet all sorts of people from the high and mighty to the gutsiest battlers. Not long after we arrived in England, we encountered one of the most unlikely cricket teams on earth. They were a side who, on paper, were more out of place than Warney at a nutritionists' convention. Three months before, one of their bowlers, Steve Aranda, held another teenager in his arms as he bled to death by the side of a road in Los Angeles. This group of kids had been brought together by their dreadlocked mentor Ted Hayes, who loves cricket almost as much as he loves helping the disadvantaged.

A few years ago he tried to get some of the poor kids in his part of LA to try their hand at the foreign game of cricket, and lo and behold, not only did they take a shine to it, they found the discipline and the concentration required gave them a focus in life

THE SECOND TEST—LORDS

that had previously been missing. Ted did a remarkable job with his players, taking them from the streets of LA to the hallowed turf of Lord's and even on to Buckingham Palace for tea with Prince Edward. London must have seemed like an alien planet to those kids from the mean streets of America.

For the groovers in our tour party, London was a whole world of entertainment. Michael Slater, his wife Stephanie, Brendon Julian and Adam Gilchrist all went to see INXS at Wembley Arena and Warney got guitarist Tim Farris tickets to the Lord's Test and gave him a ride on the team bus.

Another interesting man I met at Lord's was the son of the Sultan of Brunei and he's about as keen a sporting fan as you could ever hope to find. I visited his house at Hampstead with Stephen, Shane Warne and Ian Botham. Beefy's a real good mate of the Sultan's son and coaches him in cricket. While we were hanging out there, Viv Richards dropped in for a hit of tennis and Javed Miandad and Jansher Khan, the squash champion, all turned up.

The young Sultan loves talking about sport and he turned on a great feed for us. Let me tell you, he has a pretty flash joint and it's only one of a number of palatial homes he owns. His dad is the richest man in the world and I guess his son is probably the second richest. They have even more cash than Bill Gates and sport is their passion.

The Sultan's son goes around on a handicap of three and when he's not playing golf he's having a hit on his tennis court, or polo grounds. He'll often fly in people like Viv for a couple of weeks just to talk about sport. Ian Botham and the young Sultan get on famously, but I was glad the talk at the dinner table didn't get around to charity. Beefy had been threatening to get some of the

175

Aussies to shave their heads in a fund-raiser and since I'm quite attached to my hair I was glad the topic didn't come up. Dinner at the Hampstead mansion was a welcome break from what was the most frustrating time of the tour for us.

After we'd been swamped at Edgbaston and hung out to dry by the British press, we travelled up to Trent Bridge for the game against Nottingham, but most of it was washed out. It was a case of rain, rain, more bloody rain. Still, there was enough play for Matt Elliott and Stephen to score centuries and for Michael Bevan to make an unbeaten 75, hitting the slow leftie Usman Afzaal over the pavilion for six along the way. Paul Reiffel—just off the plane—snared 3–15 and gave a taste of just how much he would revel in the heavy atmosphere so hospitable to swing bowlers.

The Nottingham match started disastrously for me on the third day, even before I'd faced a ball. I had a race to listen to back home and Little Ricky was 15 not out resuming his innings with Matty Elliott. It was 11 am in England and 8 pm back home in Sydney where my horse Clever Kiwi was going round at Harold Park. We're not supposed to have mobile phones in the dressing-rooms, so I thought I'd go to the toilet and have a listen to the big race. First I took Ricky aside and said, 'Listen, I've got this race on, whatever you do don't get out in the first over.'

'Yeah, yeah,' he said, giving me every indication that he was planning to be out in the middle for the duration. But sure enough when I really needed him to put a big innings together for me, he was out l.b.w. in the first over.

There I was, sitting in the toilet with a mobile phone to my ear, listening to Clever Kiwi charging home. I was sprung like a kid caught having a smoke at the back of the demountables. I had to

THE SECOND TEST—LORDS

hang up the phone with 400 metres left to run and take my place in the middle. Clever Kiwi ended up running fifth. The next week he ran second at 14–1.

Ricky might have spoilt the race for me at Nottingham, but as the tour went on he became a lot more reliable with the bat. And through the remaining matches, Pistol would hold one end tight, always keeping the Poms under pressure. In the next match against Leicestershire, Pistol took six wickets in tandem with Glenn McGrath. At Leicester, we also encountered James Ormond, who took 6–54, bowling with a lot more curry than he did for Alan Crompton's Sydney University club last year.

And so, on to Lord's.

The hallowed ground might be the Mecca of cricket for the purists, but it is not an easy place for batsmen and technically it is a long way short of the world's best ground. The wicket slopes by more than two metres. For the Second Test, we found ourselves batting on a strip that had been remade in 1994 with Broughton loam. Obviously the wicket hadn't formed properly because there were cracks in it from the start of the match, with some areas hard and some soft.

Glenn McGrath took to the wet conditions like a duck to water, eclipsing the record innings bowling feat of Bob Massie, who just happened to be at the ground with a WA Cricket Association tour party. Glenn hadn't been bowling that well in the early part of the tour and had given the crowd the one-finger salute at Lord's during the one-dayers, after they got stuck into him when Ben Hollioake cut loose. But he regained his rhythm and pace against Leicester in what was our first important victory of the tour, and in the Lord's Test he opened fire on a wicket that suited him. It was the performance of a lifetime, but in all honesty I've seen him bowl that well quite often without getting the same results. At Lord's, he just put the ball on the right spot and that was good enough on the day. He hit the bat hard and bowled accurately and when he does that, Big Glenn is always going to trouble the batsmen. He was starting to look more and more like Curtly Ambrose all the time, with his exceptional bounce and consistency.

Before the series, I tipped Matt Elliott to score the most runs for Australia and he certainly set about achieving that with a debut century at Lord's. It's not a bad place to get your first Test ton and for Matt it is just the start of many more that must surely follow.

England were certainly prepared to keep up their momentum after their performance at Edgbaston. Mike Atherton had his new OBE and was leading England in a Test for the 42nd time, passing Peter May's record. The Poms were going into the match on the back of three successive Test victories, which was in itself a record of sorts for them. It was also their chance to win their first Ashes Test at the ground since 1934, when Hedley Verity, who later died of wounds in an Italian prisoner-of-war camp during the Second World War, took 14 wickets in a day against a side that included Bradman, McCabe and Woodfull. That match had been England's first victory over Australia there in 40 years and so, facing us in 1997, they had a pretty dodgy record to overcome.

Geoff Boycott spurred them on. 'Australia are in big trouble,' he wrote, 'and now I would back England to win the series.'

Shame I couldn't get some of his cash.

The Lord's Test saw Prime Minister John Howard, an unabashed cricket fan whose love for the game was nurtured by Alan McGilvray's radio broadcasts in the 1940s, drop into the

THE SECOND TEST—LORDS

Australian rooms for a few minutes and then do a spot with the ABC as a guest commentator. Needless to say Mr Howard was a little more reserved in his comments than a guest commentator for the BBC, one Mr Jeff Thomson, who sent shocks through the producers as he once did England's batsmen, letting fly with an assortment of choice words within his first few minutes at the mike.

England were riding high from their First Test victory. Lord MacLaurin, the British cricket boss, had written individual letters to each member of the side praising them for their efforts in Birmingham and commending their polished image of matching hats and no stubble. And, even though Michael Atherton shuns publicity and fame, a benefit dinner for him at the London Hilton on the eve of the Lord's Test raised about $80,000 with $22,000 coming from the bat with which he hit the match-saving 185 not out at the Wanderers. Maybe he should have kept the bat because England sure could have used that sort of performance as the series against us wore on.

The first day's play at Lord's was washed out and it was like rain on England's parade. The ECB had to give back $1.3 million in ticket money and when play resumed on Day 2, the Poms looked nothing like the side that completely outplayed us at Edgbaston. They were plundered by Big Glenn, who hit them right between the eyes even before they knew what had happened. He took 8–38 and England were all out for 77. The English press were in raptures after Edgbaston, but it didn't take them long to put the boot in at Lord's.

'Pig shooter Glenn McGrath murdered England with the best Test bowling ever by an Aussie in this country,' wrote Geoff Sweet

179

in the *News Of The World*. 'McGrath's hobby is firing at pigs in the outback. Yesterday the big boar hunter had Mike Atherton's men squealing. Sad England lasted only 42.3 overs for their lowest score at Lord's this century. Athers' slap-happy fieldsmen mucked up an amazing five catches plus a couple of run-outs and a tough stumping chance as the rampant Aussies finished the day on 131–2. Memories of England's sizzling First Test triumph soon fizzled out.'

In the same paper, Richie Benaud wrote: 'The truth is that England looked as bad with the bat and in the field as they were magnificent at Edgbaston. McGrath took full advantage of those strange pitch conditions and looked a Rolls-Royce performer rather than the second-hand sedan we saw in the First Test. McGrath is one of the finest fast bowlers Australia has produced during the last 20 years.'

Richie can say that again.

The name Glenn McGrath now goes on the Lord's dressing-room honour boards for eternity, even though it was already there in temporary fashion at lunchtime on the first day after Geoff Marsh had written it on tape and stuck it up. His bowling figures eclipsed both Bob Massie's 8–53 and Hedley Verity's 8–43. 'I had been thinking of my first ball at Lord's for weeks and weeks,' Glenn told the papers. 'I'd never even set foot here before this tour, but I soon found out that the aura of this ground is amazing. It's the home of the game and this ranks with the greatest act of my career. It's certainly a long way from my childhood in the small town of Narromine. With my rhythm back I just concentrated on a better line and length than at Edgbaston. With the slope at Lord's and the sort of pitch we played on, something was going to happen if you put enough balls in the right place.'

There were six rain interruptions on Day 2 and only 21 overs bowled, but in a 10-over burst, Glenn gave the Poms a taste of what to expect for the rest of the match. He dismissed Mark Butcher, Mike Atherton and Alec Stewart as England collapsed to 3–13. We nearly had four wickets, if not for the fair play of Ian Healy. Contrary to what Brian Lara might say, Heals is a very fair player and when he scooped up an edge off Graham Thorpe with the score at 3–14, it looked like wicket No. 4.

Heals tumbled to his left and came up with the ball in his hands. I thought it was a legitimate catch, but umpire David Shepherd was uncertain if it carried and while he consulted with umpire Venkat, Heals ran over to say that while some blokes in the slips cordon thought it carried, others weren't sure.

So Heals ran over and said, 'Shep, a few of the boys thought it was all right but I don't think I caught it.'

Shepherd said later, 'I thanked him and then he asked me what decision I was giving. I looked straight at him and said: "not out".' Shepherd then joined in with a capacity crowd of 28,000 to applaud the act of good sportsmanship from our keeper. 'That's what cricket needs,' Shepherd remarked. 'It was a marvellous effort.'

'Strewth! An Honest Aussie,' proclaimed the *Daily Star* newspaper.

When play resumed on Day 3, Thorpe was finally out for 21 in one of two wickets Pistol took from the Nursery End, while Pigeon was wreaking his havoc. But those 21 runs made Thorpe the top scorer for the Poms in their 77. It was England's lowest total at Lord's since 1888, when the most successful bowling partnership in history—Charlie 'The Terror' Turner and Jack 'The Fiend' Ferris—skittled England for 45. When Pigeon snared Nasser Hussain, the score was 6–62 and our hero had started a spell of 5–12 from 34 balls. Obviously, Pigeon had learned a lot from his chats with Dennis Lillee and was now attacking the crease more.

'Dennis thought I lacked energy,' Glenn said later, celebrating his landmark performance. 'He was probably right. I was running up too fast and today I slowed things down and hit the crease harder. My rhythm was back.'

At the end of the third day, we had lost Tubby and Greg Blewett but Matt Elliott was on 55 and I was on 26. At 2–131 and with England having dropped five catches, missed two run-outs and with John Crawley having to deputise behind the stumps for Alec Stewart nursing back spasms, we still thought we were a big chance of winning the match. So long as the rain held off. But it was a bit like the Extra ad I did on TV, with the rain coming down non-stop and we didn't go out to the crease again until 5.40 pm on Day 4.

With little time to set up a big total we threw our bats at everything, only this time the English held their catches. I was out top edging a ball off Andy Caddick for 33 and Warney, Stephen and Michael Bevan all went cheaply. But Matt Elliott finally cracked it for his Test century, hooking and driving everything to reach the ton just before 7 pm and repeat the feat of his look-alike, Bill Lawry, in his first outing there in 1961.

Matt eventually blasted one to Crawley at deep backward square leg off Caddick to be out for 112 and came off to see his name taped on the Lord's honour board. His innings had included 20 boundaries and he had picked a great place to score a debut Test

THE SECOND TEST—LORD'S

hundred. I could only rue the fact that on the previous tour, I was out for 99 at Lord's in a high scoring Test that, ironically, also saw Atherton fall a run short of his century. As time was running out, Matt cracked three fours off Gough and suddenly realised he was a show to hit three figures. 'I was half asleep,' he said later. 'I'd been cooped up in the dressing-room playing cards for three hours non-stop and there was no time for a warm-up. To be honest, I was a bit dozy going out to bat, yet look what happened.'

It was probably appropriate that Matt's blitzkrieg batting came after a lightning strike. At dawn that day, John Jameson, the assistant secretary of the MCC and a former England batsman, felt lightning hit the end of his red and yellow umbrella while inspecting the ground. 'It certainly got the pacemaker racing a bit,' he joked.

On the fifth day we put England back in straight away, hoping to repeat the first innings chaos. But this time England held firm and an opening stand of 162 by Atherton and Butcher saved the match, though I'm sure without the rain we could have won. Atherton was really the key. Butcher was dropped early and played and missed quite a bit but Athers led by example, finally being out, hit wicket, to Mike Kasprowicz on 77. Warney ruined Butcher's hopes for a Test ton when he spun a ball sharply through the gap between bat and pad. England batted out the rest of the day and it was Australia's first drawn match in 19 Tests. But the tide had turned. More and more Edgbaston seemed like an aberration. England no longer held the whip hand.

The Third Test—Old Trafford

'We allowed the Aussies to dominate us. Now we will have to play like stink to win.'

COACH DAVID LLOYD LAMENTING SOME ENGLISH BATTING THAT WAS ON THE NOSE

The bond between twins has fascinated doctors and scientists, mystics and intellectuals for thousands of years. Siblings who grow together before birth are linked by that mysterious bond that stretches beyond the womb for the rest of their lives. Stephen reckons that he's almost psychic when it comes to me; his younger brother by a whopping four minutes.

He reckons that in the West Indies in 1995 when Curtly Ambrose was running in to bowl, he had a premonition that I'd be caught-behind that very ball. Sure enough, I was. A few years before that, when he was in America and I was on tour in Sri Lanka, he had a dream that I would make a pair of ducks. And I did. (Why couldn't he dream me up a double century now and then?) There were plenty of examples of the unspoken communication between Stephen and I when we were kids. Sometimes I'd get a toothache and then he'd get one too, or sometimes I knew exactly when he was going to get sick.

My father says that the two of us have dragged each other upwards over the years through the competitiveness we showed from the first days of backyard cricket. While that is true, I don't think we try to outdo each other any more, but rather we concentrate on our own games. There is not that much difference between our games really. It's just that he has refined his style a little more.

People say that, for twin brothers, we're distant and some have even suggested that we don't get on. While we mightn't live out of each other's pockets like some twins, you have to remember that we see each other far more than most brothers would, go out to functions together far more than most brothers would and, in a sense, work together nine or ten months of the year. We're really just like normal brothers except that we see each other all the time. It's like Stephen said, when asked why we didn't room together on tours: 'We had nine months in the same womb and then 16 years in the same room, why the hell would we want to room together now?'

Not that there isn't a bond between us. Stephen still has premonitions about me and I can see what's going to happen in his future. I can often tell what shot Stephen is going to play to the next ball.

At Old Trafford, Stephen's twin centuries, made in difficult conditions, were the final straw that broke England's back in the series and established our dominance again over the old enemy. Those big totals put us onto the winning path and we never looked back until the Ashes were safely in our grasp yet again.

THE THIRD TEST—OLD TRAFFORD

After the frustration of Lord's, it was more of the same for a while with rain reducing our time in the middle. The match against Oxford was abandoned without a ball being bowled. It was so wet that we couldn't even practise. We organised a racquetball contest instead. The first prize was no gym work for the rest of the tour and the second was no gym work for a week. Both those prizes were my idea, but someone added a third with the bronze medal winner not having to talk to our manager, Alan Crompton, for a week. I don't know who was responsible for the third prize, but Crommo tends to talk in legalese a bit and obviously someone had copped a bit of a hammering from him around the earhole. Anyway, Crommo didn't mention the racquetball contest, so the culprit got away with it.

A prank or a bit of stirring now and then never hurts on tour but if there was one thing to cheer us up amid the gloom of an English rainstorm, it was the birth of Shane Warne's first child back in Melbourne. Warney missed the birth. He's joined a club that includes Allan Border and Ian Healy, who have had children born while on a tour of duty. Brooke Victoria Warne came into the world on June 27. Shane's wife Simone told him that the new baby was 'a little chubby, just like you'. We celebrated with the proud father over a few glasses of Dom Perignon and cigars at our Oxford hotel at 10.30 that night. Personally, I hate cigars. I reckon they taste terrible and while some of the hardier souls were sucking in the fumes, I was just puffing on them, a little dejected that I could get no takers at 100–1 for twins on the day of the birth. As you can imagine, Warney was happier than if he'd taken 20 wickets in a match and he'd been carrying the mobile close to his heart 24 hours a day in anticipation. But he didn't have much free time to

187

shop for baby clothes. Continuing with the baby news, the Bevans announced that Tracey was pregnant.

A day after our celebration at Oxford, we faced Matt Hayden's Hampshire side at Southampton. Greg Blewett was nowhere to be seen when the game was on. Eventually, he bobbed up with girlfriend Jodie, announcing their engagement. They met in Hobart 19 months earlier when Blewey had been skittled by Mustaq Ahmed and he was bowled over straight away.

At Hampshire's County Ground, Matt Hayden had been hitting centuries just about every game with his new county and after a public spar with Ian Chappell, was very keen to prove he deserved a place playing for Australia rather than against us. He didn't get the opportunity. His Queensland team-mate Mike Kasprowicz snared him for six in the first innings and Gillespie got him for two in the second during a spell of five wickets. Matt had only been awarded his county cap on the first morning of the match. Matt's had his chances with the Australian team and hasn't quite taken them, but he could still play for Australia down the track. He's a class act.

Tubby hit 109 against Hamps and I got my best score of the tour, 173, to set up victory by 133 runs. It was the perfect springboard onto Old Trafford, the ground where Jim Laker took 19 wickets in a match in 1956 and where Warney had caused so many problems for the Poms four years before, with his ball of the century against Mike Gatting. That day, Warney had claimed his first wicket in Ashes competition with his first delivery and in 1997 all eyes were on him to repeat the spell.

Peter Johnston wrote in the *Daily Mail* that, 'Unless Warne can assert himself and prove that his injured shoulder does not stop

THE THIRD TEST—OLD TRAFFORD

him conjuring up the occasional magic delivery, the Ashes are in danger of slipping through the Australian's fingers.'

Nasser Hussain in the same paper wrote that it was time 'to take sweet revenge on wily Warne.

'We have learned our lesson,' he wrote. 'This time we have a strategy to stop him and we don't intend to allow him to inflict the same kind of carnage at Old Trafford.' So much for England's best intentions.

Warney had struggled at Edgbaston with match figures of 1–137 and, following Tub's three-foot-wide bat stunt, another paper sent a young lass with a parcel of pies to approach Warney outside the hotel for a team photo, posing as a pie thrower. Needless to say, she didn't get far. Warney remarked that the difference between the ball he used to dismiss Gatting in 1993 and this tour was about 10,000 overs and four years of wear and tear. But one of the headline writers on a London tabloid from the Benny Hill school of journalism explained Shane's early struggle in England with a banner headline which said: 'Warne can't grip his balls'.

Double meaning or not, Warney admitted that part of the problem was the difference between the Kookaburra ball used at home and the Dukes ball in England. In any case, Warney had got the old loop back soon after the First Test in the match against Leicestershire, picking up 5–42. In the next match, the Lord's Test, he snared Butcher and Hussain in the first innings. At Old Trafford, his happy hunting ground, he would prove that he was just as dangerous as ever.

We were staying at the Manchester Holiday Inn, where in 1904, when the grand old joint had been called the Midland, a Mr Rolls and a Mr Royce met to form a small company manufacturing cars.

189

Maybe Warney was inspired by the setting for a vintage performance of his own.

The Test match started in typical fashion for us. Tubby won the toss for the third time in a row and bravely elected to bat on the dampest Test wicket I've seen. It was a bold gamble with England 1-up and a crucial match for us to win. When England were 1 for 70-odd in their first innings, I looked over to him in the slips and said, 'Would have been a nice toss to win, Tub'. But hats off to our skipper. He knew that the wicket would dry out and spin over the last couple of days and the gamble paid off. It looked a bit touch-and-go for a while as the skies were overcast all day and there was plenty of swing.

Dean Headley, loping in from the Warwick Road end, made as good a Test debut as I've seen, bowling with surprising pace and swing. Tubby ducked into a short ball in Headley's first over and was hit in the helmet and then caught by Thorpe at first slip off a ball that left him late. It was Headley's 18th ball in Test cricket and Tubby was out for two when the score was only nine. Unfortunately, Dean's father, Ron, didn't get to see the third-generation Headley's dream debut, since he was stuck in a traffic jam on the M6.

Ron's father, George Headley, had made a similarly impressive Test appearance at Old Trafford 64 years before. He danced and drove his way to 145 not out on the first day and finished unbeaten on 169 the next. George Headley's Test and first-class records rank him second behind Bradman in the history of batting, and he passed on his proud tradition to grandson Dean before his death in 1983. Although George saw out his days in Jamaica and his son and grandson made their home in the West

THE THIRD TEST—OLD TRAFFORD

Midlands, Dean remembers his old grandad showing him the finer points. 'He came to our home in Stourbridge and we went into our back garden and hit a few balls. I had read so much about him. He was not just my grandfather but a great cricketer.'

With Dean Headley inspiring his team-mates, we were 3–42 when I was out to Mark Ealham, but Stephen rescued the situation with some handy support from Matt Elliott and later Paul Reiffel. By the end of the first day, Stephen was 102 after hitting a boundary in the last over and we had crept to 7–224, a very handy total considering there had been rain delays of 20, 40 and 85 minutes during the day.

Stephen had earned the can of Coke he drained as he told reporters at stumps, 'That was probably the best hundred I've scored, up with the double century in Jamaica. It wasn't easy to bat out there because the pitch was very difficult. The partnership in the last hour with Paul Reiffel was crucial. I think it could be the difference between winning and losing.'

His 108 was phenomenal, considering the conditions were so in favour of their fast bowlers. Stephen mightn't play as many shots as other players—he doesn't hook or pull and doesn't hit the spinner over the top too often—but he knows his strengths and knows just how important it is to stay at the crease. Ironically, on the golf course he has trouble concentrating, has little patience and experiments with every shot there is, even if he has to invent them.

Thanks to his determination, we ended up with 235 the next morning and McGrath took Atherton's wicket cheaply. Butcher and Stewart took England to 1–74 and their Ashes hopes weren't looking too bad at one-up in the series. Then Mr Shane Warne entered the equation and England had a case of 'destruction deja vu'. He took Alec Stewart's wicket and when Heals stumped Butcher off a Michael Bevan full toss down the leg side, our great keeper had snared his 100th victim in 25 Ashes Tests. With Warney leading the charge, the Poms collapsed from 1–74 to all out 162 and Shane picked up 6–48.

Jim Holden of the *Express* wrote that Warney looked like he was in a hurry to get home to see his new baby and that could be true. He sure revelled in his revenge, giving the crowd the finger after the game. It was his way of answering all the critics in the crowd who'd baited him and all the journos who'd written him off. Ian Botham predicted that, if Warney stayed fit, he'd take 500 Test wickets. And who can argue with that?

Another critic, Colin Bateman, wrote that Warney had laid England out on an examination table and dissected them into little pieces, finding a team with a strong heartbeat but a soft underbelly. Alan Lee in the *Times* said: 'Whatever theories England have produced to counter the danger of Warne were either forgotten or ineffective. Even bowling of this soaring quality should not paralyse the minds and movements of Test-match players, but successive batsmen departed to strokes of sacrificial ineptitude.'

England coach David Lloyd looked like he'd seen the ghost of Ashes Losses Past at the end of Day 2, lamenting that his side should have been 2–400 instead of staring defeat in the face.

Warney had equalled Richie Benaud's 248 Test wickets and when I caught Caddick off his bowling the next morning he had slotted into third place on Australia's all-time wicket-takers list behind only Dennis Lillee and Craig McDermott. Richie Benaud said the Caddick dismissal was one 'of the most delightful moments I have known in the game'.

THE THIRD TEST—OLD TRAFFORD

'Warne is a model bowler,' Richie wrote, 'and we are lucky to be able to watch him these days, after the very nasty operation to his spinning finger early in 1996. His performance in this fascinating Test has been eye-catching, not merely because he has taken the wickets, but because he has bowled quite differently from the way he bowled before the finger problems. Then he spun the leg break an enormous amount and bowled the occasional top spinner and wrong 'un. Now he is bowling something like 10 per cent leg breaks and 90 per cent top spinners ... what struck me so forcibly was that England batsmen suddenly seemed to have no idea which way the ball was going!'

Thanks to Warney's bowling and then Stephen's continued batting success in the second innings, we were able to set England an absolutely unreachable 469 runs to win the Test. Stephen held the innings together like glue, coming to the crease when we were 3–39 and finally departing nearly 300 runs later. He marched towards a century he would complete the next morning, but the big talking point of Day 3 was a controversial catch by Nasser Hussain in the slips, off Robert Croft's bowling, to dismiss Greg Blewett. Umpire Venkat consulted with George Sharp at square leg and raised the dreaded digit. A slow-motion camera from the Stratford end showed the ball bouncing just in front of Nasser's hand.

That replay made the catch look suspect, but I played a good deal of cricket with Nasser at Essex and I would never call the bloke a cheat. I've never seen him cheat and I really don't believe that he would. If the ball did bounce in front of him, it would have been an honest mistake. That setback for us made little difference to the end result.

I hit 55 in the second innings, whacked Caddick for a four and a six and almost hit Croft for a six as well. It was the first Test innings in which I really got going, but Mark Ealham got one through the gate with a ball that seamed back. Ealham has a very good change of pace, but I admit I relaxed a little bit when he came on and I paid the price.

At the end of Day 3, Stephen was unbeaten on 82 and Warney was on 33. An injury to his right hand slowed his becoming the first right-handed Australian to make two hundreds in an Ashes Test after left-hander Warren Bardsley and Arthur Morris performed the double. Stephen's hand had been bruised making his ton in the first innings and for much of this memorable innings in his second turn at the crease he was literally batting with one hand. He was constantly taking his hand off the bat as he gleaned just 26 runs from 35 overs after tea. His right hand was swollen around the base of the thumb and forefinger and he needed repeated ice treatment. Despite the pain, there was no stopping his ton the next day and no stopping Australia, especially after our tail wagged like Lassie's in a closing scene, with Heals, Warney, Pistol and Dizzy all getting valuable runs.

In the *Sunday Times*, Allan Border said that if Warney was the conjurer of the side, then Stephen was the man most likely to destroy opposition morale with a moment of genius. He 'initiates the fervour, the passion, the pride. He is, unquestionably, its heart and soul.'

England made 44 in their second innings before Dizzy trapped Atherton, l.b.w., on the back foot. Atherton had earlier hooked Dizzy for six, but he couldn't go on with it against our speedster's sheer pace. Before long, Dizzy had dismissed Butcher and Hussain

THE THIRD TEST—OLD TRAFFORD

as well, and as he walked off to the team bus, he did so barefoot, his heels red raw with blisters.

In the *Sun*, John Etheridge wrote that, 'Gillespie, nicknamed Dizzy after the puffy-cheeked jazz trumpeter, took three wickets in 10 balls to slice through England's innings. And if you happen to have a brass instrument handy, blow a bloomin' great raspberry in the direction of England's batting.'

England were 5–130 overnight and were fairly quickly culled on the last day, despite a fighting 83 from the sparsely thatched John Crawley, who is said to be the next man on the Advanced Hair Studios hit list. We won the Test by 268 runs and the series was level at 1–1.

Geoff Boycott said England's batsmen had domino disease and had self-destructed like lemmings leaping over a cliff because they could not cope with pressure. 'Unless England eliminate this domino effect from their batting,' he said, 'they can wave goodbye to the Ashes.'

The Fourth Test—Headingley

'Under the southern cross I stand
A sprig of wattle in my hand
A native of my native land
Australia, you bloody beauty!'

AUSTRALIAN VICTORY SONG PERFORMED WITH PASSION IN THE DRESSING-ROOM AT HEADINGLEY

As I crash-tackled Mal Meninga in a heaving, screaming, thrashing heap of arms and legs on the floor of a bar in Leeds, I couldn't help feel an immense sense of satisfaction. We had just gone 2–1 up in the Test series by trouncing England at Headingley, and I had put one of the greatest Rugby League players of all time on the deck after he'd been skiting all night about running over the top of Jarrod McCracken, from my beloved Canterbury Bulldogs, in the 1994 grand final.

The main bar at the Leeds Holiday Inn was no place for a quiet ale on the night of 28 July 1997. The Canberra team was in town for the Super League World Club Challenge and they'd come down to celebrate our victory along with some blokes from the North Queensland Cowboys. The celebrations at Leeds were great, but unfortunately one of the North Queensland Rugby League players, Jason Death, was living it up too much. He got down to the old birthday suit when it wasn't his birthday and was promptly sent back to Townsville. His club threatened that his $250,000-a-year contract would be torn up.

Mainly, though, it was a fantastic night. The footy players joined the cricketers at the bar and we all had a ball telling each other how good we were. In the end, we decided to see if we could tackle Big Mal. Four of us—me, Stephen, Michael Slater and Mike Kasprowicz—lined up Mal as he charged from the other end of the bar, the cry of 'I've still got it' ringing in our ears. Somehow, the four of us brought the big fella down about 10 yards out from the imaginary try line, though I'm sure I wouldn't like to try wrapping myself around those ironbark-trunk legs on the football field.

Mal had created a bit of a stir at Headingley earlier in the day when he stepped out of his role as coach of the Canberra Raiders and stepped into a frock and a blue fright wig to join the Aussie supporters in the crowd. Some of the footy stars are cricket fans through and through. For instance, Laurie Daley, the Raiders captain and pride of Junee, once clean-bowled Michael Slater in a schoolboy match—a scalp he still talks about. He rarely mentions the fact that Slats had made 211 at the time and he certainly didn't bring up that point in Leeds when he was giving Warney some advice on the flipper.

The arrival of the Raiders also allowed Brendon Julian to renew his friendship with David Furner, Canberra's giant goal-kicker. As a schoolkid from Perth, BJ represented his state in under-15s Rugby League at a tournament in Canberra, and he was billeted to stay at Furner's home with big David and his old man, Don, a one-time Australian Rugby League coach.

The buoyant mood the footballers brought to Leeds reflected

THE FOURTH TEST—HEADINGLEY

the upswing in the Australian cricket camp after our victory at Old Trafford. In between the Third Test there and the Fourth in Leeds, we had three weeks to travel across the British Isles, playing five matches and seeing some of the best golf courses in the world.

A couple of days after beating England at Manchester, we were at Jesmond at Newcastle upon Tyne, where BJ, given few opportunities with the ball all tour, blazed away with the bat against Minor Counties. Their ground is very much on the small size, and the local houses and an adjoining cemetery are regularly bombed. BJ, who hit two tons for Surrey last season, came in at No. 4 for us and smashed 106 off 86 balls. His second 50 took just 15 deliveries with the last 10 balls faced reading 6, 6, 0, 1, 6, 6, 2, 4, 6, 6.

His innings helped us to a nine-run victory and Darren Berry, who replaced the injured reserve keeper Adam Gilchrist, whacked 34 in his first match for Australia. Darren played in a shirt he borrowed from Ian Healy, pads on loan from a mate in England and a tracksuit that belonged to Warney. 'The cap was mine,' said Darren, 'that's what mattered.' He had BJ take a photo of him the day he got his cap and was sleeping with the baggy green every night. Selection in the Australian XI wasn't a bad result for a bloke who was in England merely for a holiday and to do some club coaching.

Three days later, we were up in Edinburgh taking on Scotland the Brave. A crowd of 7000 squeezed into the picturesque Grange club, where Scotland will play their two home matches in the 1999 World Cup, against Bangladesh and New Zealand. It's a beautiful ground, surrounded by oak, sycamore, birch and chestnut trees and with a pavilion built in 1856. Michael Slater top-scored with

95, the same score as Scotland made for six wickets down when rain ended the match.

The best thing about being in Scotland was the chance to play at the spiritual home of golf, the 400-year-old St Andrew's, in a day organised by Coca-Cola. Ricky Ponting was cleaning up everywhere he played on tour, but it was Justin Langer, who plays off 20, Slats, who plays off 16, and Michael Bevan, who doesn't have a handicap but would probably be shooting off something like 10, who took the stableford points at the New Course. Ricky shot a 73 and if he ever gets tired of cricket, which I doubt, there might very well be another career for him around the corner. But Matt Elliott should stick to what he does best. He doesn't play a lot of golf and that's just as well. I was put together with him and the ABC commentator Neville Oliver and I didn't think we'd ever make it around after Matt got stuck in a bunker and took 23 shots to get out. It reminded me very much of Ian Baker-Finch's Snickers ad.

It was a great sense of occasion playing at the most famous golf course of them all, but it was even more exciting when we played the famous Road Hole, the 17th on the Old Course where Jack Nicklaus, John Daly, Nick Faldo, Seve Ballesteros, Peter Thomson, Kel Nagle and Sam Snead, among other legends, have all won the British Open. I strode down the historic hole with Ricky, Greg Blewett, Ian Jessup, a journo covering the tour, and a photographer.

It was especially exciting since we sneaked onto the famous course uninvited after a few drinks in the clubhouse as the sun was setting. We were lucky not to get thrown off. An official stopped us on our merry way, but we told him we were the Australian cricket team and that we were only there to do some photos. So we got away with it, played on down the 18th, and had a moment to savour for the rest of our lives.

A moment as treasured as meeting Mr Keith Miller for the very first time in my life, at the most picturesque ground I've ever seen. It was in the beautiful Oxfordshire countryside setting of Ibstone, on a private ground carved out of the forest on the estate of billionaire J. Paul Getty, son of Jean Paul, the eccentric and miserly American oil tycoon who was once the world's richest man. I thought I'd seen paradise at the Oppenheimer ground at Randjesfontein in South Africa, but Getty's playground was even better.

The younger Getty is a celebrity recluse and philanthropist in Britain, and a man who loved cricket so much that he bought Wisden. On Monday, July 14 he invited 400 guests to his private playground to see Australia against an Invitation XI that included Robin Smith, Martin Crowe, Ben Hollioake, Derek Randall, Graham Hick, Alex Tudor and Paul Strang.

Dickie Bird was one of the umpires and among the champagne and Pimms-drinking fans were Mick Jagger, his old flame Marianne Faithfull and Mick's elderly father, who recalled the day he trialled with Yorkshire and thought he was a chance until officials learned he'd been born at Chelmsford in Essex. Bob Simpson had a chin wag with Geoff Marsh, John Major was seen applauding Matt Elliott's 95 and Crowe's unbeaten 115, while the Bedser twins were reminiscing about swing bowlers of the 1940s and 1950s.

To say meeting Keith Miller was a great honour is an understatement. John Arlott called him the most exciting cricketer in the world for a decade after the Second World War, and to generations of cricketers ever since he has been a hero of mythical proportions. He was a wartime pilot who once flew halfway across Germany during the fighting just to get a close look at Bonn, the birthplace of Beethoven, one of his heroes.

I've always wanted to meet Keith and it's strange that while we both live in Sydney and I've been playing at the SCG for a dozen years, I finally caught up with him on the private ground of an American billionaire in the middle of the English countryside. I'd heard that Keith hadn't been in the best of health but he was in great spirits and very switched on. I had a good chat to him about racing, cricket and football and about his days playing Aussie Rules for St Kilda and how he and Warney hoped they could get up for the 1997 flag. Keith still follows cricket very closely and he is very knowledgeable about the modern game.

By the time we played at Ibstone, our driver Hughie Jones and the Manchester United bus had chalked up about 6000 kilometres, and there were still many more places to visit. Our next stop on the tour of the British Isles was Cardiff, where we played Glamorgan on a flat track at Sophia Gardens. The county had beaten Australia on the previous two tours, but this time were without their top three bowlers, Waqar Younis, Steve Watkin and Robert Croft. Ricky Ponting hammered their attack for an unbeaten 126 that more or less assured he'd take Bevvo's spot in the Test team. Tubby led from the front, hitting 71 from 88 balls, which included a six and nine fours.

In our second innings, the runs came from Greg Blewett and our new batting find Paul Reiffel, who both made half centuries, Pistol's runs coming after he'd taken 5–18 during a tremendous

THE FOURTH TEST—HEADINGLEY

bowling spell in the first innings. The match finished in a draw after Glamorgan's Stephen James, with knocks of 91 and 79, became the first man to make 1000 runs in county cricket for the summer.

Our next match against Middlesex at Lord's put together a rematch between Mike Gatting and Shane Warne, as Warney eyed the victim of his 'ball in a lifetime' at Old Trafford four years before. This time, Gatting played Warney with aplomb. I think everyone was waiting for Gatting to fail against Warney, or at least to start sweating blood, but he batted very well before a good crowd at Lord's. He hit 85 in the first innings and 47 in the second to put aside the ghost of Old Trafford in his final year in first-class cricket.

Mark Ramprakash, the Middlesex skipper, might have averaged just 16 in 19 previous Tests, but he did his selection chances no harm with 76 as he and Gatting put on 120. Warney was having his first bowl since a lightning visit back home to see Simone and new baby Brooke. Perhaps he was in a benevolent mood as he tossed up a few full tosses here and there.

Phil Tufnell showed none of the menace he'd display at the Oval a few weeks later and I picked up the man-of-the-match award for an unbeaten 142. I gave their spinner, Keith Dutch, a pretty rough time, hitting three sixes off him and then bowling him with one of my offies (he must have been unlucky).

The break between the Third and Fourth Tests gave everyone a chance to unwind a little and throughout the series in the few cherished days off we had, there were a myriad of diversions. The day after the Middlesex match finished, we were at Buckingham Palace, having our tea with the Queen. Geoff Marsh made sure he had a shave this time, since the last time he was over for a cuppa he forgot and didn't get the warmest of greetings from Her Majesty.

Even though we were constantly training and touring, there were many opportunities to mix with celebrities from other fields. Warney met Rolling Stone Ron Wood at an art gallery and was ringside to see England's most famous boxer Prince Naseem Hamed put on a show. Michael Slater, our resident hot rodder, led Stephen, Kasper and Ian Healy on a helicopter ride to Silverstone for the British Grand Prix. Slats is a bit of a rev-head.

Michael was certainly a forlorn figure for much of the England tour, not only because he didn't make a lot of runs, but because back home his $100,000 pride and joy, a special limited edition Mazda RX-7, got knocked off. There were only a few models like it in the world, and next to his wife Stephanie, I'd say that car was the love of Slats' life.

I don't know how Slats would have handled some of England's bonding exercises involving motor vehicles. At one stage, in preparation for battle with the Aussies, the Poms went on a camp organised by their rugby great, Will Carling. They did a similar thing before victories in the one-dayers with a three-day stint in Oxfordshire. Part of the management course they undertook involved clay-target shooting, archery and mutual trust exercises to build confidence in each other. Things such as driving Land Rovers blindfolded and relying on another bloke in the vehicle to give the directions. I can only speculate what might have happened if someone managed to get Devon Malcolm as their guide when he'd left the contact lenses at home or had Slats sitting next to them giving instructions like 'faster, faster, foot down'. As it was,

THE FOURTH TEST—HEADINGLEY

the Poms were the ones who had lost direction by the time we got to Headingley for the Fourth Test.

Headingley was the scene of two Test triple centuries by Don Bradman. It was also the ground where Ian Botham destroyed Australia in 1981 and where, in 1989 and 1993, Aussie teams made totals topping 600.

The Headingley match was embroiled in controversy before a ball was bowled with the 'Great Pitch Switch' scandal. We were upset that England's chairman of selectors, David Graveney, could have such an influence over the selection of a wicket, telling officials at the ground which strip to use four days before a Test. Graveney said the pitches were swapped because the designated Test wicket had bare patches and the replacement strip had a more even covering of grass offering more consistent bounce. Tubby rightly said selectors should not dictate which wicket to use and that the same thing would not happen in Australia. He pointed out that our previous five matches, two in South Africa and three in England, had been played on seaming wickets which would offer Warney little assistance. 'I think it's a sign England are nervous about us,' Tubby said. England brought in left-arm seamer Mike Smith as a notable change for the Test, but he had a match that he'd rather forget.

The night before the Headingley Test we went to a Japanese restaurant and Warney, our cuisine attache, got the girl serving to go next door and get him a margherita pizza instead. Not that Shane has anything against sushi, tempura or California rolls, it's just that his culinary tastes are not very broad. He lost a lot of weight and sharpened his fitness to become one of the greatest bowlers ever, but his diet doesn't extend much beyond cheese and tomato pizza, pies, chips and toasted cheese sandwiches (each to their own). At Lord's there were hundreds of plates of fantastic food at the buffet they'd put on for lunch. Every delicacy you could imagine. But Shane's no cordon bleu boy. He contented himself with a buttered bread roll filled with HP sauce.

Dizzy Gillespie might have been tucking into the teriyaki chicken at the Leeds restaurant, but two days later he was full of beans as he tore the Poms apart on their very own wicket, taking 7–37. He took his last three wickets in 11 balls without conceding a run and England lost their last seven batsmen for just 34, crashing from 3–138, to all out 172. Ian Healy said he had never kept to a faster spell of bowling.

The next day, Martin Johnson wrote, 'While Alan Crompton, their manager, saw fit to post a letter of protest to the England and Wales Cricket Board over what he perceived to be David Graveney hand-picking the pitch, Graveney can presumably expect a letter of congratulation from Jason Gillespie to plop through his letterbox this morning.'

Dizzy, the bloke who still measures out his run-up with a tape measure, had produced the best performance ever by an Aussie bowler at Headingley. Ron Reed wrote that while Dizzy, an intensely shy bloke, had hardly said boo to anyone all tour, he spoke so much at the press conference after the match that the reporters' audio tapes ran out.

Dizzy scared the tripe out of Mike Smith. The new seamer lasted two balls, showing more nimble footwork than Nasser Hussain's sister as he jumped away from the stumps. Old Trafford had seen the old heads of the Australian team save the day, but nowhere on tour was Australia's bright cricketing future better illuminated than

THE FOURTH TEST—HEADINGLEY

on this ground, where three of our best young guns Dizzy, Matt Elliott and Ricky Ponting all fired. Dizzy and Ricky are both 22 and Matt 25, and all have years and years of top cricket ahead of them.

England were three down for 106 after the rain-interrupted first day as we failed to make full use of the new ball. After a good sleep, Dizzy was dynamite on Day 2. Atherton was on 41 and shaping for a long, stubborn innings when he hooked Glenn McGrath in the air to Dizzy at long leg. England were 5–154 and lost another wicket for no additional runs an over later when Dizzy got the dangerous Graham Thorpe.

The rest of England toppled quickly, except for Mark Ealham, who was still there on eight not out despite suffering a cut eye from trying to heave McGrath over mid wicket. In reply we were 4–50 after Gough and Headley struck early and we would have been 5–50 if Graham Thorpe had held a catch at first slip off Mike Smith's third over in Test cricket. It was a regulation catch, but Thorpe muffed it. Matty went on to make 199 and we scored 9–501.

The *Express* ran a headline the next day that said simply in huge type 'Butter Fingers' and Mike Smith became more and more disheartened. The bloke who was the leading wicket-taker in county cricket with 55 at 14 apiece to that point, looked less and less like a Test bowler and everyone was wondering how come he was in the team and Andy Caddick, a tall customer who could have exploited the uneven bounce at Leeds, wasn't. That master of politeness and tact Fred Trueman, in assessing Smith's performance with the ball, reckoned his cat could have bowled better.

Matt Elliott certainly had his chances with more than a couple of catches going to ground, but his 199, together with little Ricky's 127, killed off any hopes of England mounting a come-from-behind Ashes triumph. Matt wasn't too disappointed at just missing out on a double century after Darren Gough hit his off-stump with a late swinging yorker that was aimed at leg and swerved at the last nanosecond. I commiserated with Matt a little later and pointed out that 199 might have fallen short of the big double-ton, but it was 100 runs better than my 99 at Lord's. Australia recovered from the 4–50 to finish Day 2 at 4–258 with Matt on 134 and Ricky 86.

Ricky's debut Test century followed the next day. Playing for Australia again after missing eight Tests, it was obvious that he didn't intend to miss too many more. Rain ruined most of the day's cricket and on Day 4 Matt had totalled more runs than England had in their whole first innings, just as he had done at Lord's.

With Paul Reiffel scoring a rapid unbeaten half century, England needed 330 runs to make us bat again. They looked as crook as Rookwood at 4–89 when Thorpe edged a ball from Gillespie that skidded off Ian Healy's fingertips into my waiting hands as I dived to my right. Nasser Hussain, who'd made just 58 runs in the five innings since his double century, gave the Poms some heart with 105 and together with Crawley, stretched the game out. Graham Gooch is a mentor to Nasser and was delighted with his effort. 'He's a fighter and always has been,' said Goochy. 'I've known him since he was about eight. He seems to thrive in difficult conditions. In Nasser's first season at Essex we were docked 25 points for a dodgy pitch at Southend. He made a hundred on it.'

THE FOURTH TEST—HEADINGLEY

England might have entertained dreams of Crawley or Nasser or the weather saving them on the last day. Instead, Warney got Nasser early on the final morning and the Poms lost six wickets for 50 runs. The *Express* came out on the front page of its sports section and declared in a formal apology: 'In common with other newspapers, we may have recently given the impression that England had a chance of *winning* The Ashes. We now accept that this was a mistake and would like to take the opportunity to say sorry to our readers.'

For the England players, it was time to reflect on what had gone wrong. For the Australian cricket team and the biggest, loudest bunch of Rugby League players you've ever seen, it was time to party.

The Fifth Test—Trent Bridge

'I carried on like a pork chop and really let my hair down. Some people like me, some people don't. I'm not going to lose any sleep over it.'

SHANE WARNE, AFTER GYRATING WITH THE JOY OF VICTORY ON THE BALCONY AT TRENT BRIDGE

Despite the taunts he gets over his weight, you could never mistake Shane Warne for Chubby Checker. But the world's best spin bowler was doing a pretty good impression of the 1950s rock star with his twist routine on the balcony at Trent Bridge in Nottingham. A little bit of bump and grind, a wiggle of the hips and a wicket held high above his head as a reminder of all those that England lost cheaply on the ground where Robin Hood might once have ridden.

Shane had been copping it from the English crowds from the moment he arrived in England with gold earring and sterling reputation. The spectators baited him at every opportunity and the crowds at times were quite a worry for all of us.

At Edgbaston, Matt Elliott had to wrestle back his cap from a spectator. You know the security is pretty slack when a member of the Australian cricket team is forced to roll around on the ground with a guy wearing a clown wig in order to get back his baggy green.

At Old Trafford there were several pitch invasions, including one joker in a Viking outfit. The security was tighter at Headingley with as many as 200 extra personnel, but sections of the crowd couldn't help themselves. The most unruly baited Warney relentlessly with their mouths and with T-shirts that were inscribed: 'Bog Off Fat Boy'. While a few of us privy to Shane's dietary habits could see a little bit of mirth in their attire, there was nothing funny about the lead-up game to the Fifth Test at Trent Bridge. It took place against Somerset and the tauntin' at Taunton was beyond a joke.

Somerset was an extremely unpleasant part of our tour. You don't mind the crowd having a go at you, but when it's nasty and personal and blokes are swearing at you in front of little kids, then it becomes pretty awful. Playing before English crowds can be quite frightening because there is that touch of the soccer hooligan about some of the fans and you get gibberers running onto the field after they've been drinking all day. Warney came under fire from the Taunton crowd—mostly Bristol City soccer fans—from the word go and they really got stuck into him after a fine bowling effort of 5–57. Stephen captained the team against his old county and Glenn McGrath replaced Ricky Ponting, who had the flu.

Somerset's local hero Andy Caddick took a five-wicket haul as well, which made you wonder why he was ever left out of the English team. His team-mate Keith Parsons made a speedy 71 in their first innings, but his joy was short-lived when he dropped an easy catch off Stephen at second slip, breaking his finger and giving him a premature end to the county season.

THE FIFTH TEST—TRENT BRIDGE

Brendon Julian picked up his swashbuckling where he'd left off at Jesmond and hit 71 off 50-odd balls against a pretty fair attack of Caddick, the big Dutchman Andre van Troost and BJ's fellow West Australian Steve Herzberg who he hit over the leg-side boundary three times.

The Somerset crowd attack was far more fierce than anything their bowlers could mount. Some of the spectators were foul and vicious in their taunts and Stephen demanded the umpires do something about the abuse. Police stepped in and two spectators were kicked out of the County Ground. Later, Stephen told the media that while 'sledging' among players was part of the game, foul-mouthed personal abuse of players by spectators simply wasn't cricket. 'Shane was irritated by it, but he's too good a pro to let it affect him,' Stephen said. 'The only thing damaged is the name of cricket.'

Somerset chief executive Peter Anderson said that, 'Unfortunately, these days at any big sporting event there is a handful of people whose purpose is to get completely plastered and then to make a nuisance of themselves.'

In the end, the match was abandoned after a deluge. With so much hostility from the crowd, we travelled north to Nottingham prepared for anything, armed with the AFL guernseys we'd all been given after Warney was spotted on the balcony of Lord's wearing a St Kilda jumper.

We arrived at Trent Bridge at about the same time as Sanath Jayasuriya was making 340 for Sri Lanka against India in Colombo. It just goes to show what a weird game cricket can be. You don't expect anyone to make 300 these days, but it's a very different game on the subcontinent and in many cases they are happy to have a draw. But Jayasuriya has improved so much, so quickly they'll have to have a steward's inquiry. He was averaging only about 15 in Test cricket before he made that hundred against us in Adelaide two seasons ago. But then he goes out and hits 340 and then belts 199 in the innings after that. The way Australia plays the game means we are always trying to win and on wickets tailored for a result, it's hard to imagine anyone batting like that—just bat, bat, bat.

Certainly, there were no marathons at the crease in Trent Bridge, where some of the best batsmen in the world were playing with no-one making a ton. We ended up beating England with consistency. Our victory there was very much an all-round effort, with contributions coming from the whole team.

Tubby emulated other great Ashes captains in Stanley Jackson, Monty Noble and Lindsay Hassett when he won the toss for the fifth time in a row and, riding on a wave of that success in our first innings, the top five batsmen all scored half centuries. Trent Bridge was the best Test match wicket we played on in the series. It was a good batting wicket, but there was a bit there for the bowlers too and every morning the ball would swing.

At the end of Day 1, I'd hit my best Test score for the series of 60 not out. But the next morning it was fairly humid and Caddick, over the moon at his Test recall, was particularly difficult, making the ball nip around all over the place. At 3–302 it looked like we were in store for some big scores, but the batting wasn't as easy as it looked and I put on just eight more runs before going l.b.w. to Caddick. The wicket had just enough bounce to make the little nicks carry and that's the reason no-one from either side reached three figures.

THE FIFTH TEST—TRENT BRIDGE

Adam and Ben Hollioake were called into the Test team together and while both made a few runs in England's first innings they did not prove to be England's saviours as the Poms had hoped. 'The brothers were brought in to provide an infusion of spirit,' wrote John Etheridge in the *Sun*, 'so what's it to be, brandy or gin? Adam and Ben Hollioake received a brutal introduction to Test cricket.'

England's woes were not confined to Mike Atherton's poor tossing. The Poms lost Darren Gough to a knee injury, which developed from his slamming down the front foot in delivery. Devon Malcolm, whose past record at Trent Bridge amounted to 5–320, could not create the big impression that was needed. Despite Caddick's fine bowling it was Dean Headley who had the best figures from our first innings with 4–87. In the end we made 427, with Mark Taylor top-scoring on 76, and along the way becoming the sixth Australian—after Allan Border, Greg Chappell, Don Bradman, Neil Harvey and David Boon—to score 6000 Test runs. Not a bad club to join.

On Day 2 Warney came into his own, getting rid of Atherton, Alec Stewart and Nasser Hussain. England were 4–188 at stumps, but could have been worse off after Thorpe, who had his lucky moments throughout the series, barely escaped being run out off a throw from Dizzy Gillespie at mid-on before he got off the mark. He made 53 on the third day before Warney added him to his list of scalps.

Stewart top-scored for England with 87, showing just what a dangerous bloke he can be when things go his way. He had kept wicket for a day and a half and barely had a breather before he was out in the middle again, opening the batting and having to concentrate like a hawk as McGrath, Reiffel and Gillespie fired them in. Stewart said later that he had agreed to move up the order to open the batting only for Trent Bridge and the Oval Tests because England were so desperate to level the series. 'Keeping wicket and opening is near enough impossible to do week in, week out,' he said. 'But we had to win the last two to win the Ashes, so I was prepared to do it.'

Stewart showed few ill-effects of his marathon behind the stumps. He and Atherton put on 106 before Athers was out for just 27, nicking one to Heals off a Warney leg break. But Stewart was slamming everything. His 50 came off just 69 balls and when he was finally out in the same way as his skipper, he'd made 87 off just 107 deliveries. Jason Gillespie copped the worst of it, being hit for 18 in one over.

Stewart's eventual dismissal gave us double reason to celebrate. Heals took a superb catch off a thick edge that deflected off our keeper's glove, went over his head and forced him to take it one-handed diving backwards. Fittingly, this freakish effort was his 300th catch in Tests and his 100th against the Poms.

England tried hard on Day 3, but good, tight bowling from our blokes, especially McGrath, ruined any chance they had of winning. They were all out more than 100 runs in arrears and when most of our blokes made runs in the second innings, England were finished.

In the *Observer*, Vic Marks put it in a nutshell, writing: '[England's] hopes of regaining the Ashes, briefly so exhilarating after that distant Edgbaston victory, slipped away as inexorably as the tranquil waters of the River Trent.'

And in the *Mail* on Sunday, Peter Hayter hammered in a coffin nail, 'As the cheeky bugler who struck up The Last Post under

THE FIFTH TEST—TRENT BRIDGE

lengthening shadows indicated, the position from which Australia will resume this morning means the issue of the summer has been put beyond reasonable doubt. The Ashes are remaining with Australia and, barring some kind of miracle on the next tour down-under in the winter of 1998–99, that will be the case well into the next century.'

On the fourth and final morning Heals, who was voted Man of the Match, and Ricky Ponting were devastating, adding 75 in just 12 overs. Heals smashed his 50 at better than a run a ball. He finally made 63 and the 451 England needed to win must have looked like Mount Everest to someone afraid of heights.

Their chairman of selectors, David Graveney, later remarked: 'Trent Bridge just confirmed what will happen to most teams playing these Australians on a flat pitch. They make things happen so quickly that games can run away from you. The hour on Sunday morning in which Healy took on our bowlers broke everyone's hearts.'

Atherton and Stewart were both out with the score on 25 and from there it just got worse. Graham Thorpe had a go, hitting an unbeaten 82 in just 92 deliveries, but the Poms simply folded under pressure. When the due time for stumps came around, they had already lost eight wickets and Tubby claimed the extra half hour of play to kill them all.

England were all out after having faced less than 50 overs and I had the great pleasure of catching Devon Malcolm off Glenn McGrath's bowling to give Australia the series. I just caught the ball and threw it up and didn't know where it went. A fan in the crowd retrieved it and gave it to Stephen, who is an avid collector of memorabilia.

Stephen even phoned home to make a bid for Victor Trumper's cap, which was part of the big memorabilia auction in Melbourne at the end of August. But he underestimated its value. He asked his wife Lynette to go to $8000 and it ended up selling for $28,000. Stephen and I both love our cricket souvenirs but he is certainly the more avid collector and has a share in a memorabilia company called Blazed In Glory that also employs our younger brother Dean.

The Poms were anything but blazed in glory after Trent Bridge. They hung their heads in defeat, bitterly disappointed at a capitulation that sparked a painful, if not unexpected, kicking from the press and renewed talk of Mike Atherton's imminent axing. 'Australia were simply just too good for us,' Atherton admitted. 'In the last two games the gulf has been pretty big. When they get into a big lead and start bowling in the fourth innings they are almost unstoppable. But it's not much consolation in defeat that they are such a good side. I will back us to win in the West Indies. But Australia are the best side in the world.'

Nasser Hussain said something similar in the *Daily Mail*, complaining that his team was too soft. 'This softness comes from playing county cricket, which is all lovey-dovey,' he lamented. 'No-one is sledging anyone, we are all mates out there and it's about a few cups of tea and maybe a Pimms or two afterwards. If you are out, there is always another innings in a day or so. The gap between this cosy little world and Test cricket is immense.'

Christopher Martin-Jenkins was even more hard-hitting. 'The way that England played in being bowled out in the second to last over of the extra half hour to lose the match, the series and the

Ashes in one vainglorious and lemming-like dash to destruction, was wholly out of keeping with the gritty traditions of Anglo-Australian cricket. "I want them to die for their country," said Lord MacLaurin of the attitude he hoped to see from the national team. But sane men do not go frivolously to their death. This was a reckless display which allowed Australia to take their hitherto hard-earned prize far too easily.'

Adam Hollioake, freely touted as being England's next Test captain and soon to be made their one-day skipper, did not take defeat easily. He visited the Australian dressing-room after the match to burn our victory scenes into his mind for some sort of revenge motivation. In the papers, he endorsed Athers as skipper, despite so many commentators calling for his head. 'Athers is a tough nut,' Hollioake said. 'He doesn't look the sort of bloke you'd be scared of meeting in a back alley, but anyone who's been through what he's been through and still come back is amazing. I was talking to Steve Waugh last night and he said Athers is like a bloody cockroach that you can't kill. You stamp on him but he keeps coming back.'

He sure does. We found that out in the last game of the tour.

The Sixth Test—The Oval

'This result is a dream come true. Ian Botham had a word with me yesterday morning and things clicked into place.'

ANDY CADDICK AFTER HELPING BOWL ENGLAND TO VICTORY AT THE OVAL IN A TRIUMPH REMINISCENT OF THEIR 1981 ASHES MIRACLE AT HEADINGLEY

We really didn't know what to expect as we breezed into Northern Ireland for a hastily scheduled tour match after the Fifth Test at Trent Bridge. Given the extent of news coverage over the political and religious violence there, we expected it to be a pretty frightening place. Nothing could have been further from the truth.

The most terrifying thing of the whole tour was the way Ricky Ponting tore into the golf course at the country club where we were staying at Derry, about an hour from Belfast. He shot 69. Ricky was the dominant man with the clubs for the whole tour, but in Ireland, with so many other leprechauns around, he really shone. No doubt he felt at home in the land of his ancestors with the beautiful green rolling hills of the Irish countryside around him and the warm, friendly people who greeted us wherever we went.

We even got to play at Royal Portrush, a spectacular course that had hosted the British seniors not long before on a layout which Gary Player reckons is the best links course in the world. It's perched right on the coast and even though it rained for most of the day while we were there, it was still a rich treat. On a clear day you mightn't be able to see forever, but locals reckon when the sun is shining you can see Scotland in the distance.

Ricky brought his form from the course to the cricket pitch at Eglinton, where he turned on the fireworks to celebrate being reunited with his relatives. His grandmother, Jean, left Ulster in 1938 at the age of 11 and before the match he met her sisters, Betty and Mary, who still live in Belfast. Little Ricky hit an unbeaten 117, off 89 deliveries and took 3–14 with the ball as we beat Ireland by 141 runs.

Two days later, we took on Kent at Canterbury in a match which saw Ricky hit 32 and 56 not out. We won by six wickets in what we thought would be the perfect lead-up to victory in the final Test at the Oval. Things didn't end up going exactly to plan. Dizzy Gillespie had broken down with stress fractures in his back threatening to keep him out of cricket for a season, Paul Reiffel had left early to be with his pregnant wife back home and hard-luck man Brendon Julian, who'd been struggling to get a bowl the whole tour, suffered a broken wrist just as he was on the verge of a Test recall.

The Kent match saw us call all-rounders Shaun Young and Shane Lee into the team, Shaun from Gloucestershire and Shane from Enfield in the Lancashire League. Against Kent, the pair tussled it out for the one Test spot on offer. Mike Kasprowicz, who would share the new ball with McGrath at the Oval, took the first four Kent wickets while Shane Lee mopped up the tail with

Ricky Ponting will form the backbone of Australia's batting for the next decade. Here in action during the 4th Test at Leeds

Photo: Clive Mason, ALLSPORT

Graham Thorpe is caught by yours truly at Headingly during the 4th Test. He was England's best player over the Summer.

A rare moment when I start to dominate the bowlers during the 5th Test.

The new era of cricket is upon us. Fitness is key when you are playing cricket nine months of the year. Here before the 6th Test.

An aggressive shot as I try to break free of the shackles of facing Phil Tufnell at The Oval in the 6th Test.

A long tour of England can't be done without the help and support of the wives and partners. Here the girls prop themselves up in the Team Hotel at Nottingham.

THE SIXTH TEST—THE OVAL

another four. Stephen hit 154 in his first dig to assure us of victory and Shane Lee finished the match with eight wickets. But as it turned out Shaun Young, with just two wickets in the match, was chosen, largely because he'd been playing county cricket day in, day out, while Shane Lee had been playing in a lesser competition.

After the Kent match, quite a few of the guys went to the Nigel Mansell Racing School at Brands Hatch racetrack, hoping to rev themselves up for the final spin with the Poms. Coca-Cola put on the day and while I had to miss it because of the flu the rest of the blokes were mad-keen to swap the cricket for racing helmets. They drove around in Formula Three cars after getting a lesson from Aussie driver Mark Webber. There were no surprises when Michael Slater came out with the fastest lap time, closely followed by Greg Blewett. Matt Elliott drives like he plays golf, but at least he avoided any collisions of the running-between-wickets kind, emerging only with the slowest lap time.

A day later, on 21 August, we were in south London preparing for battle at the Oval. We got together as a team and spoke about the problem we seem to have of losing the last Test of each series. After having dominated the Ashes series in 1993, we came out and lost by a big margin at the Oval. We had also lost the last Test to the Windies in Perth in 1996–97 and been defeated in the last match of both the Test series and the one-dayers in South Africa. We really wanted to make sure that we didn't blow it at the Oval where England have a pretty good record.

As it happened, we played pretty well for most of the three days the game lasted, but our poor batting in the last innings cost us the match and turned a seemingly inevitable and emphatic 4–1 series result into a much closer 3–2. It was disappointing for all of us because we wanted to put the record straight about our ability to finish off opponents. Swampy Marsh's theory is that we are not mentally switched on when we go into these dead games. It seems like we have the series wrapped up and subconsciously we switch off a little.

To be fair, England stuck to their guns and put in a super effort when the cause was lost. With the blast they received from the papers and supporters, we knew they'd be motivated for one last desperate assault.

At the Oval, England finally won a toss, but it looked like their luck had run out altogether at 2–24, with Atherton and Butcher both dismissed. Atherton was out 10 times in the series and Glenn McGrath snared him on seven of those occasions, dominating him in the same way he manhandled Brian Lara. With the England skipper's scalp in the first innings at the Oval, Big Glenn had taken 150 Test victims. That wicket also gave him his 31st of the series, matching the milestone Dennis Lillee achieved on his first tour of England 25 years before.

The Poms eventually made 180 but only because tailenders Andy Caddick and the new seam bowler Peter Martin had a go at the end, both hitting sixes in what was a case of trying to patch up a dam wall with a finger. The *Express* ran photos of the whole England team with a simple headline: 'Why Don't They All Resign?'

Adam Hollioake showed he still had a lot to learn about Test cricket when he shouldered arms to a leg-break from Warney which pitched on the middle stump and went straight through to bowl him. The *Mirror*, showing its customary restraint, screamed, 'Spineless! Gutless! Hopeless!' It ran a computer-generated photo

THE SIXTH TEST—THE OVAL

of Atherton in a naval uniform giving a farewell salute on a sinking ship with the accompanying words 'Captain Calamity goes down the plughole'.

Mark Ramprakash, the Middlesex skipper, is sometimes a brilliant player, but has a dodgy Test record. He came into the side in place of John Crawley, who I think was unfairly dropped. Ramprakash was another being touted as a replacement for Atherton, but he did his claim to the top job little good when he made just four before Blewey picked him up at short leg, off McGrath. Glenn was the destroyer, taking 7–76.

Victory appeared a formality, with us 2–77 in reply at stumps. England coach David Lloyd admitted his team was lacking confidence. 'We have once again been blown away,' he said. 'Both Michael Atherton and myself feel badly let down by what went on out there in the middle today. There is no hiding place for captain or coach. But you have to temper criticism with the belief that we are still in this match.'

They sure as hell were. As good as Glenn's figures were after his spell of sustained accurate pace bowling, Phil Tufnell's 7–66 was even better. Tufnell gave the best bowling performance I've seen from him. It was a good wicket to bowl on, with a quite powdery surface and the ball turned almost from the word go. Tufnell put the ball in the right spot and let it do the rest. He has often been criticised for bowling too negatively—just coming in over the wicket and bowling into the bowler's footmarks. At the Oval, though, he bowled aggressively around the wicket, attacking the batsmen and with good control.

In Australia's game against Middlesex, he did nothing out of the ordinary. He bowled over the wicket to me in that game with a very defensive field of four men on the leg side. I said in the paper the next day that I didn't think that was the way to play first-class cricket, bowling a foot outside leg stump with four guys on the leg-side boundary. You just couldn't hit the ball anywhere. But to his credit, he bowled very well at the Oval in what was his first five-wicket haul in 20 Tests.

Tufnell had been in the England squad for the start of all five previous Tests against us, only to be culled at the last minute and sent on his way. At the Oval, across town from his home ground at Lord's, he made up for lost time. It was a performance that propelled Tufnell back into the international cricket spotlight after years in the doldrums following an explosive start to his career against the Windies on the Oval and another haul of seven wickets in Christchurch soon after.

The Sixth Test was a massive personal triumph for a bloke who has ridden waves of adulation and despair throughout a stormy career. 'Tufnell has never charted an untroubled course through cricket, or life,' wrote Michael Henderson in the *Times*. 'He was expelled from Highgate School, and instructed to "cut off that ponytail" when he joined Middlesex.

'On a particularly fraught tour of Australia two winters ago, when he was the victim of some outrageous abuse from the crowd, he spent a night in the secure unit of a mental hospital and there was serious talk of sending him home. Away from the cricket, there have been some "domestics", culminating in a visit from his then father-in-law, who brought a brick with him.'

Just as well the bloke didn't bring a cricket bat with him or Tufnell would have tied him in knots. Thanks to his bowling for England, the Oval Test was still anyone's after two days of cricket.

THE SIXTH TEST—THE OVAL

Thanks largely to rearguard action from Ricky Ponting and Shane Warne, we had made 220 in spite of Tufnell's bowling and were helped by some sloppy English fielding. Poor old Shaun Young got a taste of just how tough Test cricket can be. He got to bowl just seven overs in England's first innings and lasted just two deliveries before Tufnell got one to zip out of the rough, take his glove, and land in Alec Stewart's mitts.

After his seven-wicket haul, Tufnell marched off the pitch to a standing ovation and took off up the stairs to the dressing-room for 'a fag and a cup of tea'. He says he has cut down on the smokes, but still has about five a day. He said he was hoping the England batsmen would 'whack the ball round a bit' in their second innings to give him a spell. It didn't look like that was going to happen when England lost Atherton and Stewart to Mike Kasprowicz early in the innings. I managed to snare Butcher l.b.w. with the score on 26 and England looked in danger. They stumbled to be 3–52 at stumps.

On the third day of this fascinating, see-sawing match, Warney elected not to rest his strained right groin muscle and instead bowled off a shortened run, still producing enough mystery to get two wickets. Hussain went in the first over of the morning going after the wounded, but still dangerous, bowler; hitting him to Matt Elliott.

Thorpe and Mark Ramprakash put together 79, with Thorpe getting the only half century of the game. Ramprakash tried to join him, but when he was on 48 he recklessly tried to smash Warney out of the ground and only succeeded in giving Heals another stumping. It was a savage blow to England's hopes because at that stage they needed every run they could muster to set us a decent score. The wicket of Ramprakash brought about an immediate collapse that had the press ready for a crucifixion. Kasper mopped up the tail as England lost their last four wickets for three runs and he took the well-deserved figures of 7–36.

We needed just 124 to win the series 4–1 and come home having been victors in a thoroughly one-sided Ashes campaign. But, you know what happened.

Matt Elliott padded up to Devon Malcolm's third delivery and the rot set in. We were 5–54 when Heals and Ricky Ponting put together what looked like a match-winning partnership, but Tufnell and Caddick were riding a tidal wave of adrenalin. Peter Martin took a great running catch with the sun in his eyes to stop another Warney fightback and at 5.25 pm Glenn McGrath lobbed a Tufnell delivery to Thorpe at mid-off and England had scored a remarkable victory. They had also saved a great deal of face. Our innings had lasted just 33 overs and England's triumph was greeted with a capacity crowd serenading the team with 'Swing Low, Sweet Chariot'.

Writing in the *Guardian*, former England paceman Mike Selvey said 'Tufnell and Caddick were a pair of alchemists who turned base metal into a victory of purest gold. Low scoring matches continue to represent a chink in Australia's armour that otherwise is virtually impregnable.'

Tufnell guzzled Veuve Cliquot from the bottle, fag in hand, lopsided grin splitting his cheeky face. 'It was good fun,' he told reporters. 'We were disappointed with our low score, but all the lads sat down and said we could do it, especially if we took some early wickets with the new ball.'

Mike Brearley wrote that it was a reminder of England's

incredible Botham–Willis-inspired victory at Headingley in 1981 when the Poms won by 18 runs. David Norrie wrote in the *News Of The World* that Caddick had never charged into the wicket with such passion after his pep talk from Botham.

Mike Atherton had saved his job and a remarkable series had ended with a thrilling match. Tufnell had joined Johnny Briggs and Frank Woolley as the only slow left-arm bowlers to have taken 10 wickets in an Oval Test against Australia. The early finish cost England something like a million bucks in ticket sales, but no-one from their camp was whingeing. As expected, the headline writers changed tack completely. 'Clown Prince is King' they said of Tufnell, 'England Rise From The Ashes', 'England Seize The Day'.

Even the *Express*, who had called for all the England players to resign, published this little notice.

'Due to a typographical error a headline in our edition on August 22 suggested England's cricketers "should resign". This should in fact have read: "Why don't they all re-sign".'

All Good Things

'They won the Ashes fair and square and should have the right to display them for Australian people to see.'

LORD JEFFREY ARCHER

And so another tour had ended and Australia had won another series against England. Really, I believe there is a bigger gap between the two teams than the final score suggested.

Before the tour, I had made the comment about England's players not being tough enough for Test cricket and the only time they won was when they played contrary to that rule. In the main, my tipping wasn't bad. On the eve of the tour I said Matt Elliott would make the most runs and I predicted we'd win 4–1 if we played well or 3–2 if we were a little below our best. I wish I could carry that talent for forecasting into the TAB every weekend.

England proved to be a disappointment for me as far as racing went. I never made it to the track. Not once. We were so busy touring and training that our days off never coincided with a race meeting where we were. I was confined to listening to races from Harold Park on the mobile phone in the dressing-room toilets or picking up the Fairfield trots on 2KY over the mobile on a Monday morning in England at 7.40. At least I finally won some money off Ricky Ponting, taking Davis Love for the US Open on the last day when he tipped Justin Leonard.

On the cricket field, it was a lot easier to predict a winner. The major difference in the two teams was that we were a little more consistent in our fielding, we had a couple of dead-set match winners in Glenn McGrath and Shane Warne, we took more catches, showed more discipline in line and length with our bowling and did the simple things better.

In the main, our batsmen showed more application and we were willing to hang around and build partnerships that sapped the opposition's morale. We still have aspects of our game to work on. Our recent one-day record could certainly be better and we still seem to lose the dead rubber matches. But the mood in the camp is at an all-time high.

Much of the credit for that must go to Tubby Taylor and Swampy Marsh. The major differences between Swampy and our previous coach, Bobby Simpson, is that Geoff is more into the fitness side of the game. He expects a high level of fitness from the players and is always emphasising that. He is not much older than a few of us in the team, so we all relate very well to him. We go out to dinner with him quite a bit and find it easier to relate to someone who was playing with us not that long ago. Even though he's no longer occupying the crease for us, Swampy's role in us winning the Ashes can't be underestimated.

Again the debate rages over whether we should actually bring home the Ashes urn. Supporters for the move include Prime Minister John Howard and the English novelist, parliamentarian and cricket buff Jeffrey Archer. Personally, it doesn't worry me either way, but I suppose in every other sport the winners get to take the trophy home, and in cricket we don't. But while there's no doubting the Ashes urn has a proud heritage, the actual trophy is not the most awe-inspiring prize in sport. It's not something you can carry on your shoulders as you run around the outfield. You could actually fit it into your top pocket.

After 110 days of hard work, what really mattered was that we won the thing and won it well.

Australia v. England

This is my report card on the performances of all the players involved in the Ashes Tests and the Texaco one-day series.

AUSTRALIA

MARK TAYLOR
6 TESTS   317 RUNS AT 31.70 (AV.)   HIGHEST SCORE: 129
2 ONE-DAYERS   18 RUNS AT 9.00   HS: 11

Rescued his career at Edgbaston, top-scored for Australia at Trent Bridge and was batting well at the Oval by the end of the series. In that final match, he really seemed to have hit his straps, playing some good pull shots and hitting them off his legs. I think he found form as the tour went on. He was just about gone if he didn't make runs in Birmingham. He certainly called well at the toss with five in a row and overall he captained the side well as an inspirational leader.

MATTHEW ELLIOTT
6 TESTS   556 RUNS AT 55.60 HS: 199 (2 CENTURIES)
1 ONE-DAYER 1 RUN AT 1.00

He really has grown into a top player with a very good technique. He still tends to play the hook shot too much and that gets him into a bit of trouble now and then. Overall, the Ashes campaign was a struggle for batsmen, but Matt stood out from the pack with a great series.

GREG BLEWETT
6 TESTS   381 RUNS AT 38.10 HS: 125 (1 CENTURY)
0 WICKETS FOR 17
1 ONE-DAYER 28 RUNS AT 28.00
0 WICKETS FOR 12

Greg had a good steady series after his initial ton at Edgbaston. He had a couple of bad decisions go against him in the last Test but came into his own as a very attacking player. He can change the flow of a game very quickly. I'm sure he would have liked to have scored a few more runs but overall he would have been fairly happy with his results.

MARK WAUGH
6 TESTS   209 RUNS AT 20.90 HS: 68
1 WICKET AT 16.00
3 ONE-DAYERS 131 RUNS AT 43.66 HS: 95
1 WICKET AT 33.00

I had a disappointing tour but at least I topped the bowling averages. It was one of those tours where I just seemed to get a few good balls early on and I nicked a couple off the glove. When I got the two 50s, I should have gone on to make big scores. But aside from that, I don't think I did too much wrong. I thought I played well in the Texaco series, but I was a little off the boil in the Tests.

STEPHEN WAUGH
6 TESTS   390 RUNS AT 39.00   HS: 116 (2 CENTURIES)
0 WICKETS FOR 76
3 ONE-DAYERS 60 RUNS AT 20.00   HS: 24
0 WICKETS FOR 42

I think Stephen would have been a little disappointed with his form as well. If you take out those magnificent centuries at Old Trafford, he had only an average series. But to get two centuries on that wicket in Manchester was outstanding. He hit 75 up at Trent Bridge as well, but most of the other performances were less than his usual.

RICKY PONTING
3 TESTS 241 RUNS AT 48.20 HS: 127

He had a point to prove after being dropped last summer and he did it. Ricky has heaps of ability and for a young bloke, a very solid temperament. His was a tremendous innings at Headingley and a great partnership with Matt Elliott. It is brilliant to watch him batting and he is going to be a top player for many years.

MICHAEL BEVAN
3 TESTS 43 RUNS AT 8.60   HS: 24
2 WICKETS AT 60.50 BEST: 1–14
3 ONE-DAYERS 146 RUNS AT 73.00 HS: 108 NOT OUT
1 WICKET FOR 70

He scored a heap of runs in the one-dayers but just couldn't get going in the Tests. A couple of short balls did him in, which is really weird because I've never seen him get out to the short ball in first-class cricket in NSW. When he gets to Test cricket, he seems to get out a lot. It's just a hurdle he has to overcome. I believe he is one of the best one-day cricketers in the world. He only needs some confidence in himself and he'll be right again to play Test cricket.

IAN HEALY
6 TESTS   225 RUNS AT 25.00   HS: 63
25 CATCHES, 2 STUMPINGS
3 ONE-DAYERS   51 RUNS AT 17.00   HS: 27

He broke more records on this tour and was generally magnificent behind the stumps taking some freakish dismissals. His batting and keeping combined to give him the Man-of-the-Match award at Trent Bridge when we won the series. I guess we just won't fully realise how good the bloke is until he's gone.

SHANE WARNE
6 TESTS   188 RUNS AT 18.80   HS: 53
24 WICKETS AT 24.04   BEST: 6–48
3 ONE-DAYERS   20 RUNS AT 10.00
1 WICKET AT 129.00   BEST: 1–39

At the start of the tour, it was very cold and we were playing on wet wickets that simply did not suit the spinners. But as soon as he got a bit of help from the pitch, Shane became, if not unplayable, then very hard to get away. Despite the criticism early in the tour, he's as good as ever. The operation and the wear and tear have made hardly any difference. Give him the right conditions and he'll win the match for us nine times out of 10.

PAUL REIFFEL
4 TESTS 179 RUNS AT 59.66 HS: 54 NOT OUT
11 WICKETS AT 26.63 BEST: 5–49

Looking at his performances it's hard for people to imagine that he wasn't one of the first selected for the tour. Maybe not being chosen in the initial squad might have shaken Pistol up a bit. Not getting into the team at the start made him put in a big one when he got the chance. His attitude was spot-on right from the time Tubby first threw him the ball up at Nottingham. He got wickets straight away in the overcast conditions. Pistol had missed a few games with injuries before this tour and the selectors were obviously worried about his fitness for a long tour. But he's a pretty good bowler to be leaving at home and he'd be in most Test teams if not all. His batting was the best I've ever seen and he topped the averages for the whole team.

JASON GILLESPIE
4 TESTS 57 RUNS AT 11.40 HS: 28 NOT OUT
16 WICKETS AT 20.75 BEST: 7–37
3 ONE-DAYERS 9 RUNS AT 9.00 1 WICKET AT 136.00

We were all so disappointed that he was injured again. When he's fit and well, he has to be one of the fastest bowlers in the world, if not the fastest. He tore through the Poms at Headingley with savage pace and he and Glenn McGrath are shaping up as a lethal combination for some time.

GLENN McGRATH
6 TESTS 25 RUNS AT 12.50 HS: 20 NOT OUT
36 WICKETS AT 19.47 BEST: 8–38
3 ONE-DAYERS 1 RUN
3 WICKETS AT 41.66 BEST: 2–34

An awesome performance. He was a bit short of a gallop at Edgbaston and in the early county games because he didn't quite have his rhythm. But once he got into stride he just didn't bowl any bad balls and broke some impressive records. He is now getting into the Curtly Ambrose class of fast bowlers, though he needs to have the longevity of Curtly to really be in that elevated company. Curtly is a great fast bowler who has taken 300 Test wickets, while Glenn has only got 150. If Pigeon can snare another 100 wickets then we can say he's as good as the big West Indian. But he's got to keep taking wickets for a few more years to be bracketed in that class. At present, he's probably bowling as well as Curtly.

MICHAEL KASPROWICZ
3 TESTS 21 RUNS AT 5.25 HS: 17
14 WICKETS AT 22.14 BEST: 7–36.
3 ONE-DAYERS 45 RUNS NOT OUT HS: 28 NOT OUT
3 WICKETS AT 41.66 BEST: 1–27

He was very unlucky early in the tour when he beat a lot of batsmen, but didn't get the wickets. Then Paul Reiffel came over and kept him out of the side. All Mike really needed was a confidence lifter and the seven wickets at the Oval will boost him to big things.

MICHAEL SLATER
2 ONE-DAYERS 18 RUNS AT 9

After the one-dayers, he just couldn't get a crack at it. The weather made it difficult for batting and it was a very hard tour for Slats as he was given limited opportunities to show his form. He tried to remain his usual cheery self and always led the celebrations.

His greatest successes probably came off the field. He showed outstanding form in a race car at Brands Hatch and won 240 quid in the footy tipping contest. Tubby came second and earned 120 and I snuck into third, despite a protest, with 60.

I think Stephanie Slater had already spent the money before it hit Slats' pocket.

ADAM GILCHRIST
2 ONE-DAYERS 86 RUNS AT 43.00   HS: 53

His tour was cut short with injury, but in the one-dayers he again showed what a good clean striker of the ball he is. Adam's a top one-day batsman with plenty of potential for the Test arena. He just has to wait his turn.

JUSTIN LANGER
1 ONE-DAYER 29 RUNS AT 29.00

Like Michael Slater, he didn't get much of a run and it is frustrating for him to constantly tour and hardly get a look-in. I suppose it's a lot better than missing the tour altogether. Justin remains a magnificent team man.

SHAUN YOUNG
1 TEST 4 RUNS AND NO WICKETS

It was a dream selection for Shaun. He bowled pretty well, though he didn't get a long haul with the ball. He must think batting for Australia is hard work after nought at Kent and the Oval, but finally he got off the mark.

ENGLAND

MIKE ATHERTON
6 TESTS   257 RUNS AT 23.36   HS: 77
3 ONE-DAYERS 118 RUNS AT 59.00   HS: 113 NOT OUT

He would have been disappointed with his Test batting, averaging in the low 20s. He looked good at the start of the series, but Glenn McGrath got him again and again. Glenn is the type of bowler who doesn't let too many batsmen off the hook and the wickets in the main were very bowler-friendly. It was the sort of series in which the batsmen who did get runs almost always had a slice of luck go their way, invariably with dropped catches. But Michael Atherton didn't have much luck go his way, he lost confidence and in the last couple of Tests he wasn't moving his feet at all.

As far as the Test captaincy of England is concerned, I don't really see anyone else who could lead England in the Tests. The Poms' choices are limited to probably only Nasser Hussain and Alec Stewart and Alec's 33 or 34, so he's not a long-term proposition. I think Atherton did a reasonable job as captain, given the players he had to work with. I think he has the respect of the players and he possesses a good cricket brain. But after losing five of the six tosses, he certainly has to work on that area of his game.

ALEC STEWART
6 TESTS 268 RUNS AT 24.36 HS: 87
23 CATCHES
3 ONE-DAYERS 126 RUNS AT 42.00 HS: 79
2 CATCHES, I STUMPING

He had a similar season to Mike Atherton with similar performances in the Tests and one-dayers. His Test batting must have been disappointing for him, but he has never been a big performer against Australia. He always looks a good player, striking the ball well, but he seems to get out a lot when you least expect him to. He is such a sweet timer of the ball when he's going and such a danger man because he can score so quickly, but he tends to struggle against Warney. Overall, I think it was a disappointing series for him.

GRAHAM THORPE
6 TESTS   453 RUNS AT 57.78 HS: 138
3 ONE-DAYERS 127 RUNS AT 127.00 HS: 75 NOT OUT

He was voted England's Player of the Series, but there was talk that he was going to be axed before Trent Bridge. He scored a century supporting Nasser Hussain at Edgbaston, but I think the turning point in his series came at Trent Bridge when he was run out for nought and given not out.

If he'd gone for no score then that would have been the end of him, but instead he made a scratchy 50 and in the second innings got another half century. Overall, I think he's their best batsman. He's a positive player who likes playing his shots.

NASSER HUSSAIN
6 TESTS 431 RUNS AT 39.18 HS: 207

His double century at Edgbaston was one of the best innings I've seen and he scored a ton at Headingley to boost the aggregate. But apart from those scores he fell away in the other matches and Warney got him a few times.

Nasser is a good competitor even if he does have a suspect technique in the way he squares up to the quick bowlers. He can also play and miss a lot and the ball often finds the edge of his bat.

ADAM HOLLIOAKE
2 TESTS 51 RUNS AT 12.75 HS: 45
2 WICKETS AT 27.50 BEST: 2–31
3 ONE-DAYERS 123 RUNS (NOT LOSING HIS WICKET) HS: 66 NOT OUT
4 WICKETS AT 20.50 BEST: 2–22

Big things were expected of this bloke with many commentators anointing him as the England saviour and the new Botham. It's certainly not his fault that he didn't deliver everything that was expected of him. His first-class career in England is nothing out of the ordinary. He averages 40-odd with the bat and has taken very few wickets with his medium-pacers so it's not realistic to say he should take over from Atherton as Test captain of England simply on the basis that he likes to have a go.

He showed plenty of heart in the one-dayers and played very well, hitting the winning runs in each match. Test matches, however, are a different story with a very different pressure and to be honest he didn't look up to it. The shot he played at the Oval when he let a ball go that hit his stumps demonstrated that to some extent he could crack under pressure.

MARK EALHAM
4 TESTS   105 RUNS AT 35.00   HS: 53 NOT OUT
8 WICKETS AT 23.87   BEST: 3–60
ONE-DAYERS   4 WICKETS AT 27.00   BEST: 2–21

I thought he was very much underrated by the critics and by the selectors. In fact, I thought he was one of England's better players in the Tests. He was just about the hardest batsman to dismiss and he was very much under-bowled by Mike Atherton. He had a good change of pace and his medium-pacers were often hard to handle as I found out more than once. I thought he was bloody stiff to get dropped after Headingley.

ROBERT CROFT
5 TESTS   75 RUNS AT 9.37   HS: 24
8 WICKETS AT 54.87   BEST: 3–125
3 ONE-DAYERS 2 WICKETS AT 53.00   BEST: 1–39

He changed his appearance more than Lon Chancy as the season wore on. He looked good in the one-dayers and First Test and in the field he really looked swift, running me out in the one-dayer at the Oval. He bowled well at Edgbaston, turning the ball quite a bit, but after that victory for England he seemed to lose his confidence and his deliveries stopped spinning. By the time of his last appearance at Trent Bridge, he was a shot duck with the bat and his fielding started to slow up. He was very much a different player at the end of the series than he was at the start.

DARREN GOUGH
4 TESTS   17 RUNS AT 2.83   HS: 10
16 WICKETS AT 31.93 BEST: 5–149
3 ONE-DAYERS 7 WICKETS AT 17.00 BEST: 5–44

Darren is England's best bowler—the bloke who makes things happen. He comes up with the wickets when they're needed more than anyone else. He is probably their fastest bowler when he wants to be. He was always a danger for us, but his season was curtailed with a knee injury.

DEAN HEADLEY
3 TESTS   39 RUNS AT 9.75   HS: 22
16 WICKETS AT 27.75 BEST: 4–72
1 ONE-DAYER   1 WICKET AT 36.00

He used his 195 centimetres to great effect with the ball and performed superbly at Old Trafford in his Test debut and in the next match at Headingley. But I think he was carrying injuries at the end of the series because he definitely went off the boil a little bit. I think he'll be a good bowler for England for quite a while. He has deceptive pace, he keeps the ball up and is very gutsy when he bats, getting behind the ball and really having a lash.

MARK BUTCHER
5 TESTS   254 RUNS AT 25.40 HS: 87

I thought he was harshly treated. He was just starting to find form and the selectors dropped him for Trent Bridge and then expected him to do well straight after they brought him back for the last Test at the Oval. He was starting to look good at Headingley when they cut him. He is one of the many English cricketers with family in the game. His father, Alan Butcher, is a former Test player who is now coach of Essex and Mark is married to Mickey Stewart's daughter. He's also a bit of a groover with the electric guitar.

BEN HOLLIOAKE
1 TEST 30 RUNS AT 15.00 HS: 28
2 WICKETS AT 41.50 BEST: 1–26
1 ONE-DAYER 63 RUNS AT 63.00

This kid has a lot of talent and for a 19-year-old is a pretty cool customer. But it's too much to expect great things from him considering his age and the fact he has hardly any first-class experience. I didn't think he was ready for Test cricket against us, but he will develop into a good player who can bat, bowl and field.

JOHN CRAWLEY
5 TESTS 243 RUNS AT 30.37 HS: 83
1 ONE-DAYER 52 RUNS AT 52.00

I thought he was unlucky to get dropped for the Test at the Oval and he was unlucky getting caught off the boot by Greg Blewett at Headingley. Crawley looked good to me at the crease. But he had a couple of pieces of bad luck go against him and was out of the team.

ANDY CADDICK
5 TESTS 59 RUNS AT 9.83 HS: 26 NOT OUT
24 WICKETS AT 26.41 BEST: 5–42

He bowled really well, on wickets that suited him. When he had the bat in his hands he was aggressive, hitting the ball hard from his great height of 200 centimetres. Put Gough, Caddick and Headley together and you have a very good bowling side.

DEVON MALCOLM
4 TESTS   12 RUNS AT 3.00   HS: 12
6 WICKETS AT 51.16   BEST: 3–100

At times he bowled quickly against us but he has lost a bit of pace from his glory days. He can't bat and he can't field so if you're going to have someone like that in the team, then he is going to have to get a lot of wickets. I can't see Devon doing that any more. He's probably more consistent in his bowling than I've seen him, but not as quick.

PHIL TUFNELL
1 TEST   1 RUN AT 0.50
11 WICKETS AT 8.45   BEST: 7–66

Before the series I made the comment that he was a weak player who bowled defensively. But he made me eat my words at the Oval in the best performance I've seen from him.

MARK RAMPRAKASH
1 TEST   52 RUNS AT 26.00   HS: 48

He certainly looked a good player and is one of the top performers in the county game. But when he comes out to the crease he looks nervous and under pressure, no doubt because he's made low scores in past Test matches and has felt the bite of the axe. But if he gets one or two good scores, I think he'll get the confidence to go on and make some big runs for England. He has a good technique and plenty of ability.

PETER MARTIN
1 TEST 23 RUNS AT 11.50 HS: 20
0 WICKETS FOR 51

He was a typical English seamer, not really quick, but able to swing the ball. He bowled reasonably well, but was not the sort of player who looked like he could run through a side.

MIKE SMITH
1 TEST 4 RUNS AT 4.00
0 WICKETS FOR 89

He only had the one game at Headingley and after Matt Elliott was dropped off his bowling, he seemed to lose a lot of sting. If that catch had gone his way, he might have kicked on, but his bowling didn't really measure up to Test standard. When you consider that he was the leading wicket-taker in county cricket at that time, it illustrates the gulf between the county scene and the Test arena.

PHIL DeFREITAS
2 ONE-DAYERS 0 WICKETS FOR 82

Past his use-by date.

GRAHAM LLOYD
3 ONE-DAYERS 22 RUNS AT 11.00

Fielded well in the first one-dayer at Headingley, but nothing marvellous after that.

ASHLEY GILES
1 ONE-DAYER 0 WICKETS FOR 48

A slow leftie. He did nothing of note.

CHRISTOPHER SILVERWOOD
1 ONE-DAYER   0 WICKETS FOR 44

A fast-medium bowler, he was hammered for 44 runs off six overs and not seen again during the tour.

NICK KNIGHT
2 ONE-DAYERS   16 RUNS AT 8.00   HS: 12.

He was given out l.b.w. playing the same shot in both games. He had a good season the year before, but couldn't match it against us.